Specially to

Stephanie,

Have Fun !!

8/12/2011

THE BEST OF
CHEF WAN

DEDICATION

" We can live without Friends
We may live without Books
But civilized man cannot
Live without Cooks!"
—Bulwer-Lytton

This book is specially dedicated to my mother on her 80th birthday.

The publisher wishes to thank Living Quarters (M) Department Stores Sdn Bhd, Parkson Corporation Sdn Bhd and New Convox Sdn Bhd for the loan of tableware used in this book.

Editor: Jolene Limuco
Designer: Steven Tan
Photographer and Food Stylist: Pacino Wong of You Studio
Food Preparation: Sally Teh Guat Kim

Published by Marshall Cavendish Cuisine
An imprint of Marshall Cavendish International

Other Marshall Cavendish Offices:
Marshall Cavendish International. PO Box 65829 London EC1P 1NY, UK • Marshall Cavendish Corporation. 99 White Plains Road, Tarrytown NY 10591-9001, USA • Marshall Cavendish International (Thailand) Co Ltd. 253 Asoke, 12th Flr, Sukhumvit 21 Road, Klongtoey Nua, Wattana, Bangkok 10110, Thailand • Marshall Cavendish (Malaysia) Sdn Bhd, Times Subang, Lot 46, Subang Hi-Tech Industrial Park, Batu Tiga, 40000 Shah Alam, Selangor Darul Ehsan, Malaysia

Marshall Cavendish is a trademark of Times Publishing Limited

National Library Board, Singapore Cataloguing-in-Publication Data

Wan, Chef, 1958-
The Best of Chef Wan. – Singapore : Marshall Cavendish Cuisine, 2011.
p. cm. ISBN : 978-981-4328-43-2

1. Cooking, Asian. I. Title.

TX724.5.A1
641.595 -- dc22   OCN712629310

Printed in Malaysia by Times Offset (M) Sdn Bhd

THE BEST OF
CHEF WAN

Marshall Cavendish
Cuisine

CONTENTS

INTRODUCTION

I started cooking when I was 13 years old, assisting my aunts and neighbours at weddings and special occassions. It was through this that I started appreciating the beauty of Malaysian food and its variety. Over the years, I have entertained friends, celebrities, ministers, sultans and represented Malaysia as a food ambassador. I have also hosted hundreds of cooking shows and written a few cookbooks. It is only natural that I compile all my favourite Malaysian recipes in a book.

In *The Best of Chef Wan*, you will find classic recipes from all over Malaysia. The dishes include home-cooked favourites and popular street food. The latter is an important part of the country's food culture. Today, these dishes have become part and parcel of our daily lives. I often hear other celebrity chefs, cookbook authors, editors and food writers comment that Malaysia has the best selection of cuisine found nowhere else. It makes me proud to be part of such a rich culinary culture!

Many of the dishes found here are my all-time favourites. You can imagine how difficult it was for me to choose which recipes to share. This is why I have included over 130 recipes! With this book, I hope to inspire every one to cook for their families and friends. Here you will find a range of Malaysian dishes from Nyonya Laksa, Mee Rebus, Soto Ayam, Chilli Crab to Chicken Pongteh, all of which have been perfected in my own kitchen. You will also find recipes for Thai and Indian dishes that have become popular in Malaysia.

These days, many of us do not have the luxury of time to cook an elaborate meal at home. Therefore, I have written these recipes so that they can be whipped up with little effort, but I promise you that the results are simply *sedap*!

About Malaysian Cuisine

Malaysian cuisine is representative of Malaysia's multicultural heritage. Each ethnic group in Malaysia has its own type of cuisine. However, most local dishes have been adapted to reflect the union of different flavours from various ethnic groups.

Rice is a staple in Malaysia and you will find that most of our favourite dishes are best enjoyed with a plate of rice. A typical Malaysian meal would include a meat dish, a vegetable dish and perhaps a soup. These dishes are enjoyed communal style and laid out on the table where each diner is allowed to help himself to any amount he likes. The recipes in this book are enough to serve four to six people. I hope that this will encourage you to cook these delicious Malaysian dishes to share with your family and friends!

MEAT

MEAT

MALAYSIAN SATAY WITH PEANUT SAUCE

SATE MALAYSIA DAN KUAH KACANG

Beef tenderloin 1 kg (2 lb 3 oz), cubed

Chicken breast or thigh meat 500 g (1 lb 1½ oz), cut into bite-size pieces

Castor sugar 4 Tbsp

Salt 2 tsp

Bamboo skewers 60

Marinade

Lemongrass 6 stalks, bruised

Shallots 10, peeled

Garlic 4 cloves, peeled

Galangal 1-cm (½-in) knob, peeled

Ginger 1-cm (½-in) knob, peeled

Turmeric powder 1½ Tbsp

Side dishes

Cucumbers 2, cut into wedges

Onions 2, peeled and cut into wedges

Ready-made *nasi himpit* as needed

Peanut sauce

Vegetable oil 4 Tbsp

Peanuts 300 g (10½ oz), toasted and coarsely ground

Water 250 ml (8 fl oz / 1 cup)

Thick tamarind juice 4 Tbsp, made from 2 Tbsp tamarind pulp mixed with 4 Tbsp water and strained

Sugar 4 Tbsp

Palm sugar (*gula melaka*) 100 g (3½ oz)

Salt to taste

Spice paste for peanut sauce

Lemongrass 4 stalks, sliced

Galangal 1-cm (½-in) knob, peeled

Ginger 1-cm (½-in) knob, peeled

Cumin seeds 1 tsp

Coriander seeds 1 Tbsp

Ground chilli paste 4 Tbsp

- Prepare peanut sauce. Combine ingredients for spice paste in a food processor and blend until smooth. Heat the oil in a wok and fry the spice paste for a few minutes until fragrant. Add the ground peanuts, water, tamarind juice, sugar, palm sugar and salt. Simmer until thick. Set aside.

- Prepare *satay*. Combine ingredients for marinade in a food processor and blend until smooth.

- Mix the beef and chicken separately with the marinade, sugar and salt and skewer with bamboo sticks. Leave to marinate overnight.

- Grill the beef and chicken over a charcoal fire until cooked.

- Serve with cucumber, onions, prepared peanut sauce and *nasi himpit*.

GRILLED BEEF WITH MANGO
KERABU DAGING SALAI BERSAMA MANGGA

Beef ribs 300 g (10½ oz)

Dark soy sauce 2 Tbsp

Light soy sauce 1 Tbsp

Oyster sauce 1 Tbsp

Sesame oil 1 tsp

Orange ½, juice extracted

Young ginger 1-cm (½-in) knob, peeled and finely chopped

Young mangoes 2, thinly sliced

Sauce

Grated palm sugar (*gula melaka*) 2 Tbsp

Garlic 2 cloves, peeled and finely chopped

Shallots 2, peeled and thinly sliced

Fish sauce 4 Tbsp

Limes 2, juice extracted

Red chilli 1, seeded and finely chopped

Lemongrass 1, finely chopped

- Mix all the ingredients, except mangoes and sauce ingredients, in a bowl and set aside for 3 hours to marinate.

- Meanwhile, combine ingredients for the sauce in a bowl and stir well.

- To prepare salad, grill the marinated beef and then slice thinly across the grain. Put beef and mangoes on a serving bowl or plate, pour prepared sauce over the salad and toss well. Garnish as desired and serve immediately.

BEEF DENDENG
DAGING DENDENG BERLADO

Beef topside 500 g (1 lb 1½ oz), cut into bite-size chunks

Thick sweet soy sauce 4 Tbsp

Cooking oil for deep-frying

Kaffir lime leaves 3, shredded

Salt to taste

Sugar to taste

White vinegar 3 Tbsp

Spice paste

Red chillies 8, seeded and thinly sliced

Garlic 3 cloves, peeled and thinly sliced

Shallots 6, peeled and thinly sliced

- Put beef in a pot of water and boil until tender. When beef is cooked, cut into thin slices and pound well. Season beef with thick sweet soy sauce and leave to marinate for a few minutes.

- Meanwhile, combine ingredients for spice in a food processor and blend until smooth.

- Heat oil in a wok and deep-fry the beef slices until crispy. Remove beef and set aside.

- Leave about 2 Tbsp cooking oil in the wok and fry the spice paste until fragrant. Toss in the meat. Add kaffir lime leaves, salt, sugar and vinegar.

- Stir-fry for a few more minutes. Remove from wok. Garnish as desired and serve warm with rice.

STIR-FRIED LADIES FINGERS WITH MINCED BEEF
BENDI GORENG DENGAN DAGING KISAR

Vegetable oil 4 Tbsp

Minced beef 250 g (9 oz)

Ladies fingers (okra) 300 g (10½ oz), stemmed and thickly sliced

Red capsicum (bell pepper) 1, cored and sliced

Light soy sauce 2 Tbsp

Sugar 1 tsp

Spice paste

Red chillies 6, seeded

Dried prawn (shrimp) paste (*belacan*) 2 tsp

Garlic 4 cloves, peeled

Shallots 6, peeled

- Combine ingredients for spice paste in a food processor and blend until smooth.
- Heat the oil and sauté the spice paste until fragrant. Add the beef and sauté until it changes colour.
- Add the ladies fingers and capsicum and season with soy sauce and sugar. Stir-fry until vegetables are tender. Serve warm.

STIR-FRIED GINGER BEEF WITH ASPARAGUS
DAGING GORENG BERHALIA DENGAN ASPARAGUS

Beef loin steak 500 g (1 lb 1½ oz), finely sliced

Cooking oil 3 Tbsp

Garlic 4 cloves, peeled and finely chopped

Finely sliced young ginger 3 Tbsp

Asparagus spears 20, halved

Water 4 Tbsp

Red chilli 1, seeded and chopped

Chopped spring onions (scallions) as needed

Marinade

Cooking oil 1½ tsp

Salt ½ tsp

Oyster sauce 1½ tsp

Grated ginger 1 tsp

Corn flour (cornstarch) 2 Tbsp

Beef stock granules 1 Tbsp

Tabasco sauce 1 tsp

- Combine ingredients for marinade in a bowl and stir well. Rub the marinade over the beef and set aside for 3 hours.

- Heat the oil and sauté garlic, ginger and asparagus.

- Stir in the marinated beef and add water. Stir-fry the meat quickly to maintain its tenderness.

- Garnish with chilli and spring onions and serve immediately.

STIR-FRIED PINEAPPLE BEEF
DAGING GORENG BERNANAS

Beef rump steak 500 g (1 lb 1¹/₂ oz), finely sliced

Oyster sauce 2 Tbsp

Ground white pepper ¹/₂ tsp

Sesame oil ¹/₂ tsp

Chinese cooking wine (Shaoxing) (optional) 2 tsp

Corn flour (cornstarch) 2 tsp

Peanut oil 3 Tbsp

Garlic 3 cloves, peeled and finely chopped

Ginger 0.5-cm (¹/₄-in) knob, peeled and sliced

Hot bean paste 2 Tbsp

Red capsicum (bell pepper) 1, cored and diced

Beef stock granules 2 Tbsp

Plum sauce 125 ml (4 fl oz / ¹/₂ cup)

Salt to taste

Sugar 2 tsp

Freshly ground black pepper to taste

Diced pineapples 280 g (10 oz)

Coriander leaves (cilantro) as needed

- Marinate beef with 1 Tbsp oyster sauce, ground white pepper, sesame oil, wine (if using) and corn flour for 1 hour.

- Heat peanut oil in a wok and stir-fry beef for 1 minute. Scoop out the beef and set aside, leaving a little oil in the wok.

- Add the garlic, ginger and hot bean paste to the wok and stir-fry for a few minutes. Add the capsicum and beef stock granules and fry until fragrant.

- Stir in the beef. Add the remaining oyster sauce, plum sauce, salt, sugar, ground black pepper and pineapples.

- Garnish with coriander leaves and serve immediately.

TERENGGANU BEEF CURRY
KERUTUP DAGING

Cooking oil 125 ml (4 fl oz / ½ cup)

Pandan leaves 3, shredded and knotted

Lean beef topside 1 kg (2 lb 3 oz), finely sliced

Coconut milk 750 ml (24 fl oz / 3 cups), extracted from 1 grated coconut and 750 ml (24 fl oz / 3 cups) water

Dried sour fruit (*asam gelugor*) 2 pieces

Salt to taste

Sugar 1 Tbsp

Pounded roasted grated or desiccated coconut (*kerisik*) 55 g (2 oz)

Turmeric leaf 1, finely sliced

Whole spices

Star anise 2

Cardamom pods 3

Cloves 3

Cinnamon stick 2-cm (1-in)

Spice paste

Dried chillies 20–30, soaked, seeded and drained

Onions 200 g (7 oz), peeled

Garlic 4 cloves, peeled

Ginger 2-cm (1-in) knob, peeled

Coriander powder 2 Tbsp

Fennel powder 1 tsp

Cumin powder 1 tsp

Black peppercorns 15–20

- Combine ingredients for spice paste in a food processor and blend until smooth. Set aside.

- Heat oil in a wok and sauté the whole spices and pandan leaves until fragrant. Add the blended spice paste and fry until the oil separates.

- Add the beef and fry until it shrinks. Add the coconut milk together with the dried sour fruit. Simmer until gravy thickens.

- Stir in salt, sugar, grated coconut and turmeric leaf. Discard pandan leaves and dried sour fruit. Serve warm with rice.

BEEF IN RICH GREEN CHILLI CURRY
OPOR DAGING HIJAU

Vegetable oil 125 ml (4 fl oz / 1/2 cup)

Beef topside 600 g (1 lb 5 oz), diced

Coconut milk 500 ml (16 fl oz / 2 cups), extracted from 1 grated coconut and 500 ml (16 fl oz / 2 cups) water

Pea aubergines 125 g (4 1/2 oz)

Red capsicum (bell pepper) 1, cored and sliced

Basil leaves 3 sprigs + more for garnishing

Salt to taste

Spice paste

Green chillies 100 g (3 1/2 oz)

Onion 1 large, peeled

Shallots 6, peeled

Coriander roots 4

Ginger 2-cm (1-in) knob, peeled

Lemongrass 2 stalks, finely sliced

Kaffir lime leaves 2

Dried prawn (shrimp) paste (*belacan*) 1 tsp

Coriander seeds 2 Tbsp, roasted

Fennel seeds 2 Tbsp

White peppercorns 1 Tbsp

- Combine ingredients for spice paste in a food processor and blend until smooth.

- Heat oil in a wok and sauté the spice paste until fragrant. Add the beef and cook, covered, for 5 minutes.

- Pour in the coconut milk and bring to a boil. Simmer for 25 minutes. Add the pea aubergines, capsicum and basil leaves and simmer for another 3 minutes. Season with salt. Garnish with basil leaves and serve with rice.

SWEET PRINCESS BEEF
DAGING PUTERI MANIS

Ghee 55 g (2 oz)

Cinnamon stick 5-cm (2-in)

Cardamom pods 3

Cloves 4

Curry leaves 3 sprigs + more for garnishing

Garlic 3 cloves, peeled and finely chopped

Shallots 10, peeled and finely chopped

Ginger 1-cm (^{1}/$_2$-in) knob, peeled and finely chopped

Ground chilli paste 4 Tbsp

Coriander powder 1 Tbsp

Cumin powder 2 tsp

Fennel powder 1 tsp

Beef blade, knuckle or cubes 500 g (1 lb 1^1/$_2$ oz)

Water 250 ml (8 fl oz / 1 cup)

Tamarind juice 4 Tbsp, made from 2 Tbsp tamarind pulp mixed with 4 Tbsp water and strained

Salt to taste

Sugar 2 Tbsp

Potatoes 2, large, peeled, cut into wedges and deep-fried

Tomatoes 2 large, quartered

Onion 1, peeled and sliced into rings

- Heat ghee in a wok and fry cinnamon, cardamom pods, cloves and curry leaves for a few minutes. Add garlic, shallots and ginger.

- Add the chilli paste, coriander, cumin and fennel and stir-fry until fragrant.

- Add the beef and water. Stir well and simmer for 30 minutes until the beef is tender and the sauce thickens.

- Add the tamarind juice, salt and sugar. Stir well before adding the potatoes, tomatoes and onion. Cook for another 2 minutes. Garnish with curry leaves and serve with rice.

TOK WAN BEEF RENDANG
RENDANG DAGING TOK WAN

Beef topside 500 g (1 lb 1¹/₂ oz), diced

Coconut milk 1 litre (32 fl oz / 4 cups), extracted from 2 grated coconuts and 1 litre (32 fl oz / 4 cups) water

Pounded roasted grated or desiccated coconut (*kerisik*) 110 g (4 oz)

Cumin powder 1 Tbsp

Fennel powder 1 Tbsp

Salt to taste

Sugar to taste

Red chilli 1, sliced into thin strips without cutting through at the stalk, then soaked in iced water

Spice paste

Ground chilli paste 4 Tbsp

Onions 2 large, peeled

Shallots 6, peeled

Garlic 4 cloves, peeled

Ginger 3-cm (1¹/₂-in) knob, peeled

Lemongrass 4 stalks, finely sliced

Galangal 2-cm (1-in) knob, peeled

- Combine ingredients for spice paste in a food processor and blend until smooth.

- Put the beef, coconut milk and spice paste in a wok and bring to a simmer. Cook over low heat until beef is tender.

- Add the grated coconut, cumin and fennel. Continue to simmer until the sauce starts to thicken.

- Add salt and sugar and continue to cook until the beef is almost dry. Garnish with chilli flower and serve warm with rice.

THAI-STYLE BEEF IN SPICY GRAVY
DAGING GULAI SIAM

Cooking oil 4 Tbsp

Beef lean topside 400 g (14 oz)

Pea aubergines 125 g (4¹/₂ oz)

Coconut milk 250 ml (8 fl oz / 1 cup),
extracted from 1 coconut and
250 ml (8 fl oz / 1 cup) water

Kaffir lime leaves 2

Salt to taste

Sugar to taste

Lime 1, juice extracted

Spice paste

Garlic 3 cloves, peeled

Galangal 2-cm (1-in) knob, peeled

Turmeric 2-cm (1-in) knob, peeled

Dried prawn (shrimp) paste (*belacan*) 2 Tbsp

Coriander roots 2

Kaffir lime 1, zest only

Lemongrass 3 stalks

Shallots 8, peeled

- Combine ingredients for spice paste in a food processor and blend until smooth.

- Heat oil in a wok and stir-fry the spice paste until fragrant. Add the beef and stir-fry for about 1 minute, then add the pea aubergines.

- Add the coconut milk and kaffir lime leaves and simmer until meat is tender. Season with salt and sugar. Before serving, add lime juice. Garnish as desired and serve warm with rice.

BEEF IN TANGY PINEAPPLE SAUCE
DAGING MASAK ASAM NANAS

Cooking oil 125 ml (4 fl oz / ½ cup)

Beef 1 kg (2 lb 3 oz), cut into bite-size pieces

Tamarind juice 180 ml (6 fl oz / ¾ cup), made from 2 Tbsp tamarind pulp mixed with 180 ml (6 fl oz / ¾ cup) water and strained

Lemongrass 1 stalk, bruised

Galangal 1-cm (½-in) knob, peeled and bruised

Kaffir lime leaves 3, shredded

Salt to taste

Sugar to taste

Pineapple ½, peeled and sliced

Spice paste

Coriander seeds 1 Tbsp, roasted

Dried chillies 15, soaked, seeded and drained

Onions 2, peeled

Ginger 2.5-cm (1-in) knob, peeled

Turmeric 2.5-cm (1-in) knob, peeled

Dried prawn (shrimp) paste (*belacan*) 2 Tbsp

- Combine ingredients for spice paste in a food processor and blend until smooth. Heat oil in a wok and fry the spice paste for a few minutes until fragrant.

- Add the beef and stir-fry for a few minutes. When the meat shrinks slightly, pour in tamarind juice and add the lemongrass, galangal, kaffir lime leaves, salt and sugar.

- Cook until the beef is tender, then add the pineapple slices. Stir well and simmer until gravy thickens. Serve warm with rice.

BEEF AND POTATO CURRY
KARI DAGING DAN KENTANG

Cooking oil 125 ml (4 fl oz / ½ cup)

Cinnamon stick 3-cm (1½-in)

Star anise 2

Nutmeg 3

Cloves 3

Garlic 3 cloves, peeled and finely minced

Shallots 8, peeled and finely minced

Curry leaves 3 sprigs

Meat curry powder 100 g (3½ oz)

Beef 500 g (1 lb 1½ oz)

Potatoes 2, cut into wedges and deep-fried

Coconut milk 1 litre (32 fl oz / 4 cups), extracted from 1½ grated coconuts and 1 litre (32 fl oz / 4 cups) water

Salt to taste

Sugar to taste

- Heat oil in a wok and fry cinnamon stock, star anise, nutmeg, cloves, garlic and shallots until golden brown.
- Add the curry leaves, curry powder, beef, potatoes and coconut milk and simmer until meat is tender. Add salt and sugar to taste. Serve warm with rice.

PADANG-STYLE BEEF RENDANG
RENDANG DAGING PADANG

Vegetable oil 125 ml (4 fl oz / ½ cup)

Coriander powder 2 Tbsp

Fennel powder 2 Tbsp

Cumin powder 2 Tbsp

Freshly ground black pepper 2 Tbsp

Lemongrass 2 stalks, bruised

Kaffir lime leaves 2

Beef 1 kg (2 lb 3 oz), cut into thick slices

Coconut milk 1 litre (32 fl oz / 4 cups), extracted from 1½ grated coconuts and 1 litre (32 fl oz / 4 cups) water

Mixed spices (cardamom, cloves, cinnamon, star anise)

Tamarind juice 125 ml (4 fl oz / ½ cup), from 2 Tbsp tamarind pulp mixed with 125 ml (4 fl oz / ½ cup) water and strained

Sugar 6 Tbsp

Salt to taste

Pounded roasted grated or desiccated coconut (*kerisik*) 8 Tbsp

Turmeric leaf 1, finely sliced

Spice paste

Shallots 15, peeled

Garlic 6 cloves, peeled

Ginger 2-cm (1-in) knob, peeled

Turmeric 3-cm (1½-in) knob, peeled

Dried prawn (shrimp) paste (*belacan*) **granules** 1 Tbsp

Dried chillies 30, soaked, seeded and drained

- Combine ingredients for spice paste in a food processor and blend until smooth.

- Heat oil in a wok and sauté the spice paste together with coriander, fennel, cumin and ground black pepper.

- Put in the lemongrass and kaffir lime leaves and cook over low heat until fragrant.

- Add the beef and coconut milk and cook for 30 minutes until beef is tender.

- When the gravy thickens, add tamarind juice, sugar and salt to taste and grated coconut. Garnish with finely sliced turmeric leaves. Serve hot with rice.

BEEF SLICES IN BLACK SAUCE
DAGING MASAK HITAM CIK DAH

Cooking oil 6 Tbsp

Beef 1 kg (2 lb 3 oz), finely sliced

Dried sour fruit (*asam gelugor*) 3 pieces

Palm sugar (*gula melaka*) 45 g (1½ oz), grated

Water 1 litre (32 fl oz / 4 cups)

Sweet soy sauce 125 ml (4 fl oz / ½ cup)

Red chilli 1, seeded and thinly sliced

Spice paste

Powdered chilli or ground chilli paste 3 Tbsp

Shallots 8, peeled

Garlic 4 cloves, peeled

Chopped ginger 2 tsp

Lemongrass 4 stalks, finely sliced

Turmeric powder 1 tsp

- Combine ingredients for spice paste in a food processor and blend until smooth. Heat oil in a wok and sauté the spice paste until fragrant.

- Add the beef, dried sour fruit, palm sugar and water. Simmer until beef is tender.

- Stir in the sweet soy sauce and cook until sauce is almost dry. Garnish with sliced chilli and serve with rice.

BEEF AND PAPAYA IN SPICY GRAVY
DAGING MASAK GULAI KAWAH

Cooking oil 4 Tbsp

Beef 500 g (1 lb 1½ oz), thinly sliced

Store-bought coconut cream 500 ml (16 fl oz / 2 cups)

Pounded roasted grated or desiccated coconut (*kerisik*) 2 Tbsp

Salt to taste

Brown sugar 2 Tbsp

Dried sour fruit (*asam gelugor*) 2 pieces

Young papaya ½, skinned and diced

Spice paste

Dried chillies 20, soaked, seeded and drained

Meat curry powder 2 Tbsp

Mixed spice powder (*rempah masak*) 1 Tbsp

Shallots 7, peeled

Onion 1, peeled

Garlic 3 cloves, peeled

Ginger 3-cm (1½-in) knob, peeled

Galangal 2-cm (1-in) knob, peeled

Whole spices

Cinnamon stick 2-cm (1-in)

Cloves 3

Star anise 2

Cardamom pods 3

- Combine ingredients for the spice paste in a food processor and blend until smooth.

- Heat oil in a wok and sauté the whole spices until fragrant. Add the spice paste and stir-fry until fragrant and oil surfaces.

- Put in the beef and stir to coat well. Add a little water and stir well.

- Once the oil surfaces, add in coconut cream, pounded coconut, salt and brown sugar. Allow to simmer, stirring occasionally.

- Bring to the boil. Add in dried sour fruit pieces, young papaya and simmer until the gravy thickens. Serve hot with rice.

MUTTON MASALA
DAGING KAMBING MASALA

Ghee 4 Tbsp

Onions 3, peeled and chopped

Ginger 2-cm (1-in) knob, peeled and minced

Garlic 4 cloves, peeled and minced

Garam masala 1 Tbsp

Chilli powder 1 Tbsp

Coriander powder 1 Tbsp

Nutmeg 1 tsp

Fennel seeds 1 Tbsp

Leg of lamb 1 kg (2 lb 3 oz), de-boned and cut into small cubes

Tomato purée 2 Tbsp

Water 500 ml (16 fl oz / 2 cups)

Coriander leaves (cilantro) 2 sprigs, finely chopped + a few more sprigs for garnishing

Green chillies 3, seeded and chopped

Plain yoghurt 250 ml (8 fl oz / 1 cup)

Salt to taste

- Heat ghee in a pot and brown the onions, ginger and garlic.

- Add garam masala, chilli powder, coriander powder, nutmeg and fennel seeds and stir-fry until fragrant.

- Add the lamb, tomato purée and water and cook until lamb is tender.

- Once the gravy starts to thicken, stir in the chopped coriander, chillies and yoghurt. Season with salt. Garnish with coriander leaves and serve hot with chapatti, naan or rice.

MUTTON DALCA
DALCA KAMBING

Ghee 55 g (2 oz)

Meat curry powder 45 g (1½ oz), mixed with a little water to form a paste

Mutton or lamb ribs 1 kg (2 lb 3 oz), cut into bite-size pieces

Dhal 200 g (7 oz), soaked in water overnight and boiled until soft

Coconut milk 1 litre (32 fl oz / 4 cups), extracted from 1 grated coconut and 1 litre (32 fl oz / 4 cups) water

Aubergine (eggplant/*brinjal*) 1, cut into 6 pieces

Ladies fingers (okra) 6, stemmed and halved

Potatoes 2, peeled and quartered

Carrot 1, large, peeled and cut into 6 pieces

Green chillies 2, seeded and halved lengthwise

Red chilli 1, seeded and halved lengthwise

Long beans 100 g (3½ oz), cut into 3-cm (1½-in) lengths

Tomatoes 2, sliced or quartered

Tamarind juice 4 Tbsp, made from from 1 Tbsp tamarind pulp mixed with 4 Tbsp water and strained

Salt to taste

Shallots 6, peeled, sliced and fried until crisp

Spice paste

Shallots 10, peeled

Garlic 2 cloves, peeled

Ginger 1-cm (½-in) knob, peeled

Whole spices

Cardamom pods 3

Cloves 3

Cinnamon stick 5-cm (2-in)

Star anise 2

Curry leaves 4 sprigs

- Combine ingredients for spice paste in a food processor and blend until smooth.
- Heat ghee in a wok and stir-fry the spice paste with the whole spices. Add the meat curry powder and fry until fragrant.
- Stir in the mutton or lamb ribs and fry for a few minutes.
- Add the dhal, coconut milk and all the vegetables and simmer for about 30 minutes. Add the tamarind juice and season with salt.
- Just before serving, garnish with crisp-fried shallots. Serve warm with rice.

MURTABAK

Ready-made *roti canai* dough as needed

Ghee 4 Tbsp

Onions 2, peeled, 1 minced and 1 coarsely diced

Garlic 3 cloves, peeled and minced

Shallots 5, peeled and minced

Ginger 1-cm (½-in) knob, peeled and minced

Meat curry powder 4 Tbsp mixed with 3 Tbsp water to form a paste

Minced beef, mutton or chicken 500 g (1 lb 1½ oz)

Salt to taste

Sugar to taste

Eggs 3, beaten

Coriander leaves (cilantro) 1 bunch, chopped

Pickled onions

Onions 2, peeled and thinly sliced

Distilled table vinegar 500 ml (16 fl oz / 2 cups)

Sugar 1 Tbsp

- To make pickled onions, soak the onions in vinegar and sugar overnight. Before serving, drain the vinegar.

- Heat ghee in a frying pan and fry minced onions, garlic, shallots and ginger until golden brown.

- Add the curry powder mixture and fry until fragrant. Add the minced meat and stir-fry for a few minutes until the meat is well browned.

- Add enough water to cover the meat. Season with salt and sugar and leave to cook over low heat for 10 minutes until the mixture is dry.

- Cool the mixture slightly. Then dish out into a bowl and combine with the diced onion, eggs and coriander leaves.

- Take a ball of ready-made *roti canai* dough and flatten it into a square on a greased marble slab.

- Spoon part of the beef mixture onto the square dough and fold in the ends so that they overlap.

- Pinch the edges together to seal and transfer the *murtabak* to a greased frying pan.

- Cook, turning often, until the *murtabak* is golden on both sides. Serve with pickled onions and curry of choice.

POULTRY

CHICKEN IN SPICY COCONUT MILK
AYAM KAPITAN

Vegetable oil 4 Tbsp

Chicken 1, about 1.5 kg (3 lb 4¹/₂ oz), cut into 12 pieces

Coconut milk 500 ml (16 fl oz / 2 cups), extracted from 1 grated coconut and 500 ml (16 fl oz / 2 cups) water

Tamarind juice 125 ml (4 fl oz / ¹/₂ cup), made from 1 Tbsp tamarind pulp mixed with 125 ml (4 fl oz / ¹/₂ cup) water and strained

Salt to taste

Spice paste

Dried chillies 20, seeded, soaked in water and drained

Candlenuts 6

Onions 2, peeled

Shallots 15, peeled

Garlic 4 cloves, peeled

Turmeric 1-cm (¹/₂-in) knob, peeled

Galangal 1-cm (¹/₂-in) knob, peeled

Ginger 1-cm (¹/₂-in) knob, peeled

Lemongrass 3 stalks, finely sliced

Kaffir lime leaves 3, shredded

- Combine ingredients for spice paste in a food processor and blend until smooth.
- Heat oil in a wok and sauté the spice paste over medium heat until fragrant. Add the chicken, stir well and cook, covered, for about 15 minutes.
- Stir in the coconut milk and bring to a simmer, then add tamarind juice.
- Season with salt and cook until the gravy is slightly thick and chicken is tender. Serve warm with rice.

SPICY CHICKEN RENDANG
RENDANG AYAM PEDAS

Chicken 1, about 1.5 kg (3 lb 4½ oz), cut into 12 pieces

Coconut milk 500 ml (16 fl oz / 2 cups), extracted from 1½ grated coconuts and 500 ml (16 fl oz / 2 cups) water

Pounded roasted grated or desiccated coconut (*kerisik*) 110 g (4 oz)

Salt to taste

Sugar to taste

Turmeric leaf 1, finely sliced

Red chillies 2, sliced into flowers

Kaffir lime leaves a handful, shredded

Spice paste

Shallots 8, peeled

Garlic 3 cloves, peeled

Lemongrass 8 stalks, finely sliced

Ginger 2-cm (¾-in) knob, peeled

Galangal 2-cm (¾-in) knob, peeled

Turmeric 2-cm (¾-in) knob, peeled

Red chillies 6, seeded

Bird's eye chillies (*cili padi*) 5, seeded

Coriander powder 1½ Tbsp

Cumin powder 1 Tbsp

Fennel powder 1 Tbsp

Ground chilli paste 2 Tbsp

- Combine ingredients for spice paste in a food processor and blend until smooth.
- Combine chicken, spice paste and coconut milk in a pot and simmer for about 30 minutes until gravy is almost dry.
- Reduce heat and add grated coconut. Season with salt and sugar.
- Add turmeric leaf and give a quick stir before turning off the heat. Garnish with chillies and kaffir lime leaves. Serve warm with rice.

STIR-FRIED SPICY CHICKEN WITH MINT
AYAM GORENG PUDINA

Chicken breast 600 g (1 lb 5 oz), cut into bite-size pieces

Oyster sauce 1/2 tsp

Corn flour (cornstarch) 1 tsp

Sesame oil 1/4 tsp

Fish sauce 1/2 tsp

Vegetable oil 4 Tbsp

Lemongrass 3 stalks, sliced

Salt to taste

Sugar to taste

Lime juice 2 Tbsp

Mint leaves a handful, chopped + more for garnishing

Lime 1, quartered

Spice paste

Red chillies 10 large, seeded

Dried prawn (shrimp) paste (*belacan*) 1 Tbsp

Lemongrass 2 stalks, finely sliced

Ginger 1-cm (1/2-in) knob, peeled

Garlic 4 cloves, peeled

- Combine ingredients for spice paste in a food processor and blend until smooth. Remove and set aside.

- Combine chicken with oyster sauce, corn flour, sesame oil and fish sauce in a bowl and set aside to marinate for at least 10 minutes.

- Heat oil in a wok and fry the lemongrass for a few minutes. Add the spice paste and continue to fry until fragrant.

- Add the marinated chicken and fry until it is cooked through. Season with salt, sugar and lime juice. Remove from heat and toss in the mint leaves. Garnish with mint leaves and lime wedges. Serve immediately.

FRAGRANT FRIED CHICKEN
AYAM GORENG SRI WANGI

Chicken breasts 4, skinned, deboned and cut into strips

Cooking oil for deep-frying + 1 Tbsp

Lemongrass 2 stalks, finely sliced

Torch ginger bud 1, finely sliced

Bird's eye chillies (*cili padi*) 10, seeded and sliced

Tom yam **paste** 2 Tbsp

Water 4 Tbsp

Honey 1 tsp

Mayonnaise 1½ Tbsp

Kaffir lime leaves 3, central stems removed and finely sliced

Marinade

Oyster sauce 1½ Tbsp

Salt to taste

Egg 1, medium, beaten

Corn flour (cornstarch) 3 Tbsp

- Combine ingredients for marinade in a bowl and stir to mix well.
- Combine chicken with the marinade and set aside for 15 minutes.
- Heat oil in a wok and deep-fry the chicken until golden brown and crisp. Drain well on paper towels. Set aside.
- In a clean wok, heat 1 Tbsp oil and sauté the lemongrass, torch ginger bud, chillies and *tom yam* paste until fragrant.
- Add water, honey and chicken. Stir well. Remove from heat and stir in mayonnaise. Add the kaffir lime leaves and toss well. Serve warm with rice.

CHICKEN PONGTEH
AYAM PONGTEH DEGAN TAUCU

Cooking oil 6 Tbsp

Shallots 30, peeled and thinly sliced

Garlic 15 cloves, peeled and thinly sliced

Chicken 1, about 1 kg (2 lb 3 oz), cut into
  8 pieces

Preserved soy bean paste (*tau cheo*)
  3 Tbsp

Light soy sauce 2 Tbsp

Dark soy sauce 2 Tbsp

Ginger 2-cm (1-in) knob, peeled and
  finely sliced

Cloves 4

Star anise 2

Chinese mushrooms 10, soaked in hot
  water until softened then drained

Potatoes 3, peeled and halved

Water 750 ml (24 fl oz / 3 cups)

Red chillies 2, seeded and halved
  lengthwise

Green chillies 2, seeded and
  halved lengthwise

Sugar 2 Tbsp

Ground white pepper 2 tsp

Coriander leaves (cilantro) 1 Tbsp,
  finely chopped

- Heat oil in a wok and sauté the shallots and garlic until golden brown.
- Add the chicken, preserved soy bean paste, light soy sauce, dark soy sauce, ginger, cloves, star anise, potatoes and water. Stir then bring to the boil.
- Put in the chillies, sugar and ground white pepper. Reduce heat and allow to simmer for 20–25 minutes until the chicken is tender.
- Garnish with the chopped coriander leaves and serve hot.

JAVANESE FRIED CHICKEN
AYAM GORENG JAWA

Chicken 1, about 1.5 kg (3 lb 4$^1\!/_2$ oz), cut into bite-size pieces

Coconut milk 375 ml (12 fl oz / 1$^1\!/_2$ cups), extracted from 1 grated coconut and 375 ml (12 fl oz / 1$^1\!/_2$ cups) water

Tamarind juice 4 Tbsp, made from 1 tsp tamarind pulp mixed with 4 Tbsp water and strained

Salt to taste

Rice flour 55 g (2 oz)

Cooking oil for deep-frying

Spice paste

Red chillies 4, seeded

Coriander seeds 2 tsp

Candlenuts 2

Shallots 12, peeled

Lemongrass 1 stalk, finely sliced

Galangal 2.5-cm (1-in) knob, peeled

Turmeric 2.5-cm (1-in) knob, peeled

Grated palm sugar (*gula melaka*) 2 tsp

- Combine ingredients for spice paste in a food processor and blend until smooth.

- Combine chicken, coconut milk, tamarind juice, salt and spice paste in a large pot and simmer over medium heat until chicken is tender and the gravy is thick. Remove from heat and leave chicken in the gravy to marinate for at least 4 hours in the refrigerator. Remove from the refrigerator and separate chicken from gravy.

- Coat chicken with rice flour. Heat oil in a wok and deep-fry chicken pieces until golden brown. Drain well.

- Serve the fried chicken with reserved gravy on the side.

CHICKEN IN SPICY TOMATO GRAVY
AYAM MASAK MERAH

Chicken 1, about 1.5 kg (3 lb 4¹/₂ oz), cleaned and cut into 8 pieces

Turmeric powder 1 tsp

Salt 1 tsp + more to taste

Vegetable oil 250 ml (8 fl oz / 1 cup)

Tomato ketchup 125 ml (4 fl oz / ¹/₂ cup)

Green peas 70 g (2¹/₂ oz)

Onion 1, peeled and sliced

Sugar to taste

White sesame seeds for garnishing

Mint leaves for garnishing

Spice paste

Ground chilli paste 3 Tbsp

Shallots 6, peeled

Garlic 3 cloves, peeled

- Combine ingredients for spice paste in a food processor and blend until smooth.
- Rub chicken pieces with turmeric powder and 1 tsp salt.
- Heat the oil and deep-fry the chicken until golden brown. Remove and set aside.
- Leave 5 Tbsp of oil in the wok and fry the spice paste until fragrant.
- Add the chicken and tomato ketchup and cook for a few minutes.
- Add the peas and onion and season with salt and sugar. Garnish with sesame seeds and mint. Serve immediately.

STIR-FRIED CHICKEN WITH CASHEW NUTS
AYAM GORENG BERGAJUS

Cooking oil 4 Tbsp

Dried chillies 6, rinsed clean, seeded, soaked in water to soften and cut into bite-size pieces

Cashew nuts 200 g (7 oz)

Sesame oil 2 Tbsp

Finely chopped garlic 4 tsp

Chicken breast or thigh meat 400 g (14 oz) cut into bite-size pieces

Onion 1/2, medium, peeled and diced

Pineapple 55 g (2 oz) peeled, cored and diced

Green capsicum (bell pepper) 1, small, seeded and cut into bite-size pieces

Celery 2 stalks, cut into bite-size pieces

Tomato ketchup 250 ml (8 fl oz / 1 cup)

Chilli sauce 6 Tbsp

Light soy sauce 2 tsp

Sugar 2 Tbsp or to taste

Salt 1/2 tsp or to taste

- Heat oil in a wok and sauté dried chillies and cashew nuts until cashew nuts are golden brown. Remove from heat and set aside.

- Add sesame oil to the wok and reheat pan medium heat. Add garlic and stir-fry until fragrant.

- Add chicken and stir-fry briskly for 1 minute before adding onion, pineapple, capsicum and celery. Continue to stir-fry until chicken is cooked.

- Add tomato ketchup, chilli sauce and light soy sauce. Add sugar and salt to taste.

- Finally, add fried dried chillies and cashew nuts. Stir-fry until well combined and dish out. Garnish as desired and serve warm with rice.

CURRIED CHICKEN
PENCOK AYAM

Chicken 1, about 1.5 kg (3 lb 4^1/$_2$ oz),
   cut into 12 pieces

Salt 1 tsp + more to taste

Ground white pepper to taste

Cooking oil 3 Tbsp

Coconut milk 250 ml (8 fl oz / 1 cup),
   extracted from 1 grated coconut and
   435 ml (14 fl oz / 1^3/$_4$ cups) water

Turmeric leaf 1, finely sliced

Tamarind juice 1 Tbsp, made from
   1 tsp tamarind pulp mixed with 1 Tbsp
   water and strained

Sugar to taste

Pineapple 1 wedge, sliced

Basil leaves a handful

Spice paste

Red chillies 8, seeded

Bird's eye chillies (*cili padi*) 6, seeded

Candlenuts 4

Shallots 8, peeled

Garlic 2 cloves, peeled

Galangal 1-cm (^{1}/$_2$-in) knob, peeled

Dried prawn (shrimp) paste (*belacan*)
   1 Tbsp

Lemongrass 2 stalks, bruised

- Rub chicken with salt and pepper and grill in a preheated oven at 180°C (350°F) until half-cooked about 15 minutes.

- Meanwhile, combine ingredients for spice paste in a food processor and blend until smooth.

- Heat oil in a wok and sauté the spice paste until fragrant. Add coconut milk and turmeric leaf and simmer for 15 minutes.

- Add the grilled chicken and simmer over medium heat until gravy is almost dry and chicken is done.

- Add tamarind juice, salt and sugar and cook for 3 minutes. Garnish with pineapple and basil leaves. Serve immediately.

CHETTINAD CHICKEN
AYAM CHETTINAD

Chicken 1, about 1.5 kg (3 lb 4½ oz), cut into 12 pieces

Turmeric powder 1 Tbsp + ¾ tsp

Salt 1 tsp + more to taste

Cooking oil for deep-frying + 3 Tbsp

Coconut ½, grated

Onions 2, peeled and diced

Curry leaves 4 sprigs

Ginger 2-cm (1-in) knob, peeled and sliced

Garlic 3 cloves, peeled and finely chopped

Chilli powder 2 Tbsp

Garam masala ¾ tsp

Tomatoes 3, chopped

Water 4 Tbsp

Lime juice 2 Tbsp

Cashew nuts 15, lightly roasted

Lightly roasted spices

Fennel seeds 1 tsp

Cinnamon stick 3-cm (1½-in)

Cardamom pods 3

Cloves 4

- Rub chicken with 1 Tbsp turmeric and 1 tsp salt. Heat oil in a wok and deep-fry chicken until golden. Drain well and set aside.

- Finely grind the coconut together with the roasted spices.

- Heat 3 Tbsp oil and sauté onions, curry leaves, ginger and garlic until fragrant and lightly browned. Add the ground coconut mixture, chilli, garam masala, ¾ tsp turmeric and fried chicken. Sauté for a few minutes.

- Add tomatoes and water and simmer until the gravy thickens. Season with salt and lime juice. Garnish with cashew nuts and serve immediately with rice.

SPICY CHICKEN LIVER
SAMBAL GORENG HATI AYAM

Cooking oil 3 Tbsp

Onion 1, peeled and sliced

Shallots 6, peeled and sliced

Garlic 2 cloves, peeled and sliced

Ground chilli paste 2 Tbsp

Lemongrass 4–5 stalks, bruised

Galangal 1-cm (¹/₂-in) knob, peeled and pounded

Large prawns (shrimps) 300 g (10¹/₂ oz), shelled and deveined

Chicken livers 8, cut into large pieces

Long beans 300 g (10¹/₂ oz), diagonally sliced

Bean curd 4 pieces, each cut into cubes and deep-fried

Fermented soy bean cake (*tempe*) 4 pieces, each cut into 6 pieces and deep-fried

Red chillies 4, seeded and sliced

Green chillies 4, seeded and sliced

Kaffir lime leaves 2, shredded

Coconut milk 125 ml (4 fl oz / ¹/₂ cup), extracted from ¹/₂ grated coconut and 125 ml (4 fl oz / ¹/₂ cup) water

Tamarind juice 4 Tbsp, made from 3 Tbsp tamarind pulp mixed with 4 Tbsp water and strained

Glass noodles 90 g (3 oz), soaked to soften and drained

Salt to taste

Sugar to taste

- Heat oil in a wok and sauté onion, shallots and garlic until soft. Add the chilli paste, lemongrass and galangal and continue to sauté until fragrant.

- Stir in the prawns and chicken livers, then add long beans, bean curd and fermented soy bean cake. Add the chillies and kaffir lime leaves.

- Pour in coconut milk and tamarind juice and add the glass noodles. Simmer for 2–3 minutes until prawns and chicken cooked. Season with salt and sugar. Garnish as desired and serve warm with rice.

NOTE

To make chicken stock, boil chicken neck, backbones and/or wing tips from 1 chicken in 3 litres (96 fl oz / 12 cups) water and simmer for 20-30 minutes. You can also add some chopped vegetables, such as onions, carrots, celery stalks and leeks. Strain before use. Alternatively, dissolve chicken stock cubes, granules or concentrate in water and boil according to manufacturer's directions.

KUNG PAO CHICKEN
AYAM KUNG PAO

Chicken breasts 4, cut into large cubes

Oyster sauce 2 Tbsp

Corn flour (cornstarch) 1 tsp + 2 tsp mixed with 1 Tbsp water

Cooking oil 6 Tbsp

Dried chillies 8, seeded and halved

Garlic 4 cloves, peeled and finely chopped

Celery 2 stalks, diced

Red capsicum (bell pepper) 1, cored and diced

Canned bamboo shoots 55 g (2 oz), diced

Cashew nuts 20, lightly roasted

Spring onions (scallions) as needed, chopped

Sauce

Balsamic vinegar 4 Tbsp

Chicken stock 4 Tbsp

Sherry or rice wine (optional) 3 Tbsp

Hoisin sauce 2 Tbsp

Dark soy sauce 1 Tbsp

Sesame oil 1 tsp

Spicy garlic sauce 2 Tbsp

Sugar to taste

- Combine chicken, oyster sauce and 1 tsp corn flour in a bowl and set aside to marinate for 15 minutes.

- Heat 3 Tbsp oil in a wok and fry the dried chillies for 1 minute. Add marinated chicken and fry for 2 minutes. Drain chicken on paper towels and set aside.

- In a clean wok, heat the remaining oil and sauté the garlic, celery, capsicum and bamboo shoots for 2 minutes.

- Combine ingredients for sauce in a bowl and stir to mix well.

- Add fried chicken and sauce ingredients to the pan and bring to the boil.

- Add the corn flour mixture and simmer until sauce thickens. Stir in cashew nuts and garnish with spring onions. Serve immediately.

CHICKEN AND PINEAPPLE STIR-FRY
AYAM GORENG BERNANAS

Cooking oil 4 Tbsp

Chicken breast or thigh meat 500 g
(1 lb 1½ oz), cut into large cubes

Lemongrass 1 stalk, bruised

Onion 1, peeled and cut into wedges

Tomatoes 2, cut into wedges

Pineapple ¼, peeled, cored and cut into
bite-size pieces

Red chilli 1, seeded and diagonally sliced

Green chilli 1, seeded and
diagonally sliced

Kaffir lime leaves 2, torn or bruised

Oyster sauce 1 Tbsp

Fish sauce 1 Tbsp

Salt to taste

Sugar to taste

Spice paste

Dried prawns (shrimps) 4 Tbsp, rinsed,
soaked in water to soften and drained

Dried prawn (shrimp) paste (*belacan*)
1 Tbsp, dry-roasted

Ground chilli paste 3 Tbsp

Shallots 5, peeled

Garlic 2 cloves, peeled

Coriander roots (cilantro) 2

- Combine ingredients for spice paste in a food processor and blend until smooth. Set aside.

- Heat 1 Tbsp oil in a wok. Fry chicken until lightly browned. Remove and set aside.

- Add the remaining oil and reheat over low heat. Fry spice paste and lemongrass until fragrant.

- Add onion, tomatoes, pineapple, chillies, kaffir lime leaves and chicken. Stir-fry until well mixed, then add oyster and fish sauces. Adjust seasoning with sugar and salt to taste. Increase heat to medium and cook, covered, for 3 minutes. Dish out and serve with rice.

CHICKEN KURMA
KURMA AYAM

Cooking oil 180 ml (6 fl oz / ³/₄ cup)

Butter 2 Tbsp

Onions 2, big, cut into wedges

Garlic 6 cloves, peeled and thinly sliced

Ginger 2-cm (1-in) knob, peeled and thinly sliced

Curry leaf 1 stalk

Cinnamon stick 2-cm (1-in)

Star anise 1

Clove powder 1 tsp

Cardamom powder 1 tsp

Store-bought kurma powder 200 g (7 oz)

Ground almonds 1 Tbsp

Freshly ground black pepper 1 Tbsp

Water 1.5 litres (48 fl oz / 6 cups) + more as needed

Potatoes 5, peeled and quartered

Chicken breasts, 6, cut into bite-size pieces

Tomato 1, cut into wedges

Red chillies 3, seeded and halved lengthwise

Crisp-fried shallots as desired

Coconut milk 250 ml (8 fl oz / 1 cup), extracted from 1 grated coconut and 250 ml (8 fl oz / 1 cup) water

Plain yoghurt 3 Tbsp

Spring onion (scallion) 1, finely chopped

Coriander leaf (cilantro) 1 sprig

Salt to taste

- Heat oil and butter in a wok and fry the onions, garlic, ginger and curry leaf.

- Add cinnamon, star anise, clove and cardamom. Fry until fragrant.

- Add the kurma powder, ground almonds and pepper. Stir for 1–2 minutes.

- Add water, adding more as desired. Stir well and add the potatoes. Allow to simmer until the potatoes soften.

- Add chicken, tomato, chillies, crisp-fried shallots, coconut milk and yoghurt. Stir well and let it simmer until chicken is cooked.

- Add spring onion and coriander leaf. Season with salt. Serve warm with rice.

CHICKEN IN SWEET SOY SAUCE
AYAM SOS HITAM MANIS

Chicken 1, about 1.5 kg (3 lb 4¹/₂ oz), cut into 12 pieces

Salt 1 tsp + more to taste

Turmeric powder 1 tsp

Cooking oil for deep-frying

Dark raisins 85 g (3 oz)

Dark soy sauce 85 ml (2¹/₂ fl oz / ¹/₃ cup)

Tamarind juice 250 ml (8 fl oz / 1 cup), made from 1 Tbsp tamarind pulp mixed with 250 ml (8 fl oz / 1 cup) water and strained

Sugar 55 g (2 oz) + more to taste

Pandan leaves 2, shredded and knotted

Diced pineapples 280 g (10 oz)

Chopped coriander leaves (cilantro) 2 Tbsp

Spice paste

Dried chillies 15, seeded and soaked to soften

Shallots 10, peeled

Garlic 5 cloves, peeled

Ginger 2.5-cm (1-in) knob, peeled

Galangal 2.5-cm (1-in) knob, peeled

- Combine ingredients for spice paste in a food processor and blend until smooth. Set aside.

- Season chicken with 1 tsp salt and turmeric powder. Heat oil in a wok and deep-fry chicken until golden brown. Drain well and set aside. Reserve 4 Tbsp oil and discard the rest.

- In a clean wok, heat reserved oil and briefly sauté the spice paste and raisins until fragrant. Add dark soy sauce, tamarind juice, sugar and pandan leaves. Season with salt and cook until gravy thickens.

- Stir in the fried chicken and pineapples. Season with more salt and sugar if necessary. Garnish with coriander leaves and serve immediately with rice.

LEMON AND HONEYDEW CHICKEN
AYAM TEMBIKAI DAN LEMON

Boneless chicken breasts 4, about 100 g (3½ oz) each, cut into thin strips

Oyster sauce to taste

Corn flour (cornstarch) 1 Tbsp

Plain (all-purpose) flour 2 Tbsp

Egg 1, beaten

Breadcrumbs 85 g (3 oz)

Cooking oil for deep-frying

Lemon slice ½, sliced

Lemon zest a few strips

Sauce

Water 85 ml (2½ fl oz / ⅓ cup)

Lemon juice 85 ml (2½ fl oz / ⅓ cup)

Honey 4 Tbsp

Chicken stock granules 2 tsp

Light soy sauce 2 tsp

Lemon rind 1 tsp

Corn flour (cornstarch) 2 tsp

Honeydew melon 170 g (6 oz), scooped into balls

- To make lemon and honeydew sauce, combine all ingredients for sauce, except the honeydew melon balls, in a saucepan and simmer until sauce thickens. Add the melon balls and heat through. Set aside.

- Combine chicken, oyster sauce and corn flour in a bowl and set aside to marinate for 15 minutes.

- Dust the chicken pieces with flour. Dip them in beaten egg and coat with breadcrumbs. Heat oil in a wok and deep-fry chicken until golden brown. Drain and arrange on a serving platter.

- Pour prepared sauce over the fried chicken and garnish with lemon slices and zest. Serve warm with rice.

RICH CURRY CHICKEN
GULAI LEMAK AYAM

Bird's eye chillies (*cili padi*) 25, seeded and finely minced

Turmeric 3-cm (1^1/$_2$-in) knob, finely minced

Coconut milk 250 ml (8 fl oz / 1 cup), extracted from 1 grated coconut and 250 ml (8 fl oz / 1 cup) water

Chicken ^{1}/$_2$, about 600 g (1 lb 5 oz), cut into 6 pieces

Lemongrass 1 stalk, bruised

Salt to taste

Sugar to taste

Turmeric leaf 1, finely sliced

- Place all the ingredients, except turmeric leaf, in a pot and cook for about 35 minutes over low heat.
- Garnish with finely sliced turmeric leaf and serve warm with rice.

CHEF WAN'S SPECIAL ROAST CHICKEN

AYAM PANGGANG ISTIMEWA CHEF WAN

Vegetable oil 125 ml (4 fl oz/ ½ cup)

Chicken 1, about 1.5 kg (3 lb 4½ oz), quartered

Coconut milk 500 ml (16 fl oz / 2 cups), extracted from 1½ grated coconut and 500 ml (16 fl oz / 2 cups) water

Lemongrass 2 stalks, bruised

Kaffir lime leaves 2

Pandan leaves 2, knotted

Palm sugar (*gula melaka*) 55 g (2 oz), grated

Tamarind juice 125 ml (4 fl oz / ½ cup), made from 1 Tbsp tamarind pulp mixed with 125 ml (4 fl oz/ ½ cup) water and strained

Salt to taste

Store-bought coconut cream (optional) as needed

Spice paste

Dried chillies 30, soaked, seeded and drained

Shallots 20, peeled

Garlic 3 cloves, peeled

Ginger 2-cm (1-in) knob, peeled

Galangal 2-cm (1-in) knob, peeled

Cumin 1½ Tbsp

Mustard seeds 2 Tbsp

Lemongrass 2 stalks

- Combine ingredients for spice paste in a food processor and blend until smooth.

- Heat oil in a wok and sauté spice paste for 3 minutes until fragrant and oil surfaces. Add chicken and fry until half-cooked.

- Add coconut milk, lemongrass, kaffir lime leaves and pandan leaves. Bring to the boil and allow to simmer for 30 minutes until chicken is tender.

- Add palm sugar, tamarind juice and salt to taste.

- Remove chicken and place it on a baking tray. Meanwhile, cook the remaining liquid until thick. For a creamier sauce, add some coconut cream if desired.

- Glaze chicken with sauce and roast over glowing coals for 10 minutes. Turn the chicken over regularly until fragrant. Alternatively, roast chicken in an oven preheated to 180°C (350°F) for 15 minutes. Serve with rice.

CHICKEN WRAPPED IN BANANA LEAF

PEPES AYAM

Chicken 1, about 1.5 kg (3 lb, 4½ oz), cut into 12 pieces

Lime juice 1 Tbsp

Salt to taste

Tamarind juice 1 Tbsp, made from 2 tsp tamarind pulp mixed with 1 Tbsp water and strained

Spring onions (scallions) 4, cut into 2.5-cm (1-in) lengths

Basil leaves 5 sprigs

Salam **leaves** 4, shredded

Lemongrass 2 stalks, bruised, cut into 2.5-cm (1-in) lengths and shredded

Red chilli 1, seeded and finely sliced

Galangal 2.5-cm (1-in) knob, peeled and finely sliced

Banana leaves and aluminium foil for wrapping chicken

Spice paste

Turmeric 2.5-cm (1-in) knob, peeled

Shallots 5, peeled

Garlic 3 cloves, peeled

Grated palm sugar (*gula melaka*) or brown sugar 1 Tbsp

Ginger 1.5-cm (¾-in) knob, peeled

Candlenuts 55 g (2 oz)

- Combine ingredients for spice paste in a food processor and blend until smooth.

- Season chicken with lime juice and salt. Add the spice paste and mix well.

- Add tamarind juice, spring onions, basil leaves, *salam* leaves, lemongrass, chilli and galangal and mix thoroughly.

- Place 2–3 pieces of chicken on a piece of banana leaf and aluminium foil and wrap to enclose. Repeat with the rest of the chicken pieces.

- Steam chicken over boiling water for 40 minutes. Serve warm.

TANGY CHICKEN STEW
ASAM CHICKEN

Cooking oil 4 Tbsp

Chicken 1, about 1 kg (2 lb 3 oz), cut into 8 pieces

Water as needed

Store-bought coconut cream 500 ml (16 fl oz / 2 cups)

Tamarind juice 4 Tbsp, made from 1 Tbsp tamarind pulp mixed with 4 Tbsp water and strained

Pineapple ¹/₂, peeled, cored and cut into small chunks

Laksa **leaves** a handful, chopped + extra for garnishing

Aubergine (eggplant/brinjal) 1, cut into 4 pieces

Salt to taste

Sugar to taste

Spice paste

Shallots 10, peeled

Garlic 4 cloves, peeled

Lemongrass 2 stalks, sliced

Turmeric 2-cm (1-in) knob, peeled

Kaffir lime leaves 4, central stems removed

Dried prawn (shrimp) paste (*belacan*) 2 tsp, toasted

Ground chilli paste 5 Tbsp

Coriander powder 1 Tbsp

- Combine ingredients for spice paste in a food processor and blend until smooth.

- Heat oil in a pot and stir-fry spice paste over low heat until fragrant. Add chicken and stir until well coated. Cook chicken, stirring regularly, for 10 minutes. Add a little water to prevent sticking, if necessary.

- Add coconut cream and tamarind juice, then add just enough water to cover chicken. Stir through and bring to a simmer. Cook, stirring regularly, for 30 minutes.

- Add pineapple, *laksa* leaves and aubergine. Season to taste with salt and sugar. Continue to simmer until aubergine is slightly softened.

- Dish out on to serving plate and garnish as desired with extra *laksa* leaves. Season to taste with salt and sugar. Serve warm with rice.

MUM'S SAMBAL CHICKEN
SAMBAL GORENG AYAM EMAK

Chicken 1, about 1.5 kg (3 lb, 4^1/$_2$ oz), cut into 12 pieces

Turmeric powder 1 Tbsp

Salt 1 tsp

Cooking oil for deep-frying

Curry leaves 3 sprigs

Tamarind juice 4 Tbsp, made from 1 Tbsp tamarind pulp mixed with 4 Tbsp water and strained

Water 4 Tbsp

Potatoes 3, peeled, cut into wedges and deep-fried

Tomatoes 2, quartered

Salt to taste

Sugar to taste

Spice paste

Dried chillies 20, seeded, soaked in water and drained

Coriander seeds 1^1/$_2$ Tbsp

Fennel seeds 1 Tbsp

Cumin seeds 1 Tbsp

Ginger 1-cm (^{1}/$_2$-in) knob, peeled

Garlic 4 cloves, peeled

Shallots 8, peeled

- Combine ingredients for spice paste in a food processor and blend until smooth. Remove and set aside.

- Rub chicken with turmeric and salt.

- Heat oil in a wok and deep-fry chicken until just cooked. Do not let it become crisp. Drain.

- Reserve 3 Tbsp oil in a wok and discard the rest. In the reserved oil, sauté spice paste together with curry leaves for a few minutes until fragrant.

- Add fried chicken, tamarind juice and water. Cook until gravy thickens, then add potatoes and tomatoes. Season with salt and sugar and stir for 2 minutes. Serve warm with rice.

CHICKEN KUZI
AYAM KUZI

Ghee 4 Tbsp

Mixed spices (cloves, star anise, cardamom, cinnamon)

Lemongrass 2 stalks, bruised

Pandan leaves 3, knotted

Onions 2, peeled and thinly sliced

Ground chilli paste 5 Tbsp

Coriander powder 2 Tbsp

Cumin powder 1 Tbsp

Fennel powder 1 Tbsp

Raisins 250 g (9 oz)

Chicken 1, about 1.5 kg (3 lb 4^1/$_2$ oz), cut into 16 pieces

Tomato purée 5 Tbsp

Milk 250 ml (8 fl oz / 1 cup)

Rose water 250 ml (8 fl oz / 1 cup)

Saffron threads 1 tsp

Water as needed

Salt to taste

Sugar to taste

Plain yoghurt 150 ml (5 fl oz)

Crisp-fried shallots 250 g (9 oz)

Kaffir lime leaves 2–3, shredded

Ground ingredients (A)

Shallots 20, peeled

Garlic 3 cloves, peeled

Ginger 2-cm (1-in) knob, peeled

Ground ingredients (B)

Green chillies 8, seeded

Coriander leaves (cilantro) 55 g (2 oz)

Mint leaves 55 g (2 oz)

- Heat ghee in a wok and fry ground ingredients (A) together with the mixed spices, lemongrass and pandan leaves until fragrant. Add the onions and fry until golden brown.

- Add the chilli paste, powder, cumin and fennel powders, raisins and ground ingredients (B). Fry until fragrant.

- Put in the chicken and tomato purée. Cook over low heat for 15 minutes.

- Add milk, rose water, saffron and a little water. Cook until chicken is tender and the gravy is thick.

- Add salt and sugar to taste. Stir in yoghurt and cook for another 5 minutes. Sprinkle with crisp-fried shallots and kaffir lime leaves. Serve immediately.

91

FRIED CHICKEN WITH PRESERVED SOY BEANS
AYAM GORENG TAU CHEO

Chicken breasts 4, about 100 g (3¹/₂ oz) each, diced

Peanut oil 4 Tbsp

Cashew nuts 85 g (3 oz)

Red chillies 2, seeded and finely pounded

Garlic 2 cloves, peeled and finely pounded

Ginger 1-cm (¹/₂-in) knob, peeled and finely pounded

Preserved soy beans (*tau cheo*) 3 Tbsp

Chinese cooking wine (Shaoxing) (optional) 4 Tbsp

Red capsicum (bell pepper) 1, cored and diced

Yellow capsicum (bell pepper) 1, cored and diced

Courgette (zucchini) 1, finely diced

Spring onions (scallions) 2, finely sliced

Marinade

Light soy sauce 2 tsp

Corn flour (cornstarch) 2 tsp

Sugar ¹/₂ tsp

- Combine chicken with marinade ingredients and set aside for 1 hour.

- Heat oil in a wok and fry the cashew nuts until golden. Remove and set aside.

- In the same oil, sauté chillies, garlic and ginger until fragrant. Add preserved soy beans and marinated chicken. Cook until the chicken is tender.

- Add the wine (if using), red and yellow capsicums and courgette and cook for another 2–3 minutes. Toss in the fried cashew nuts.

- Garnish with spring onions and serve immediately.

GRILLED CHICKEN IN SPICY GRAVY

AYAM PERCIK

Coconut milk 1 litre (32 fl oz / 4 cups), extracted from 1 grated coconut and 1 litre (32 fl oz / 4 cups) water

Chicken 1, about 1 kg (2 lb 3 oz), cleaned and halved lengthways

Lemongrass 10 stalks, bruised

Galangal 6-cm (2¹/₂-in) knob, peeled, thickly sliced and bruised

Salt to taste

Sugar or to taste

Turmeric leaf ¹/₂, finely sliced

Spice paste

Red chillies 3, seeded

Shallots 4, peeled

Garlic 3 cloves, peeled

Ginger 2.5-cm (1-in) knob, peeled

Turmeric 2.5-cm (1-in) knob, peeled

Candlenuts 10

Fenugreek seeds 1 tsp

- Combine ingredients for spice paste in a food processor and blend until smooth. Transfer to a large pot. Add coconut milk to the pot. Stir through and bring to the boil, then simmer until oil separates to form a layer on top.

- Add chicken, lemongrass and galangal. Stir until chicken is well coated with pot ingredients. Season to taste with salt and sugar. Simmer for 30 minutes, stirring regularly until chicken is cooked. Add a little water to prevent sticking, if dry, but liquid level in the pot should always be as low as possible.

- Remove chicken from gravy and charcoal- or oven-grill it for 10 minutes, basting frequently with gravy from the pot. Place grilled chicken on a serving plate.

- Return pot to the stove and reduce remaining gravy over medium-low heat, stirring constantly, until it thickens further to the point where it will cling to the chicken when spooned over.

- Remove gravy from heat and spoon over chicken. Garnish as desired with turmeric leaves and serve immediately.

CHICKEN MASALA
AYAM MASALA

Ghee 4 Tbsp

Onions 2, peeled and diced

Cloves 2

Cardamom pods 3

Chicken breasts 3, about 100 g
(3¹/₂ oz) each, cut into bite-size
pieces

Tomato purée 2 Tbsp

Evaporated milk 150 ml (5 fl oz)

Water as needed

Salt to taste

Sugar to taste

Plain yoghurt 100 ml (3¹/₃ fl oz)

Coriander leaves (cilantro)
a handful, roughly chopped

Green chillies 2, seeded and
chopped

Spices (combined)

Coriander powder 2 tsp

Garam masala 2 tsp

Chilli powder 1 tsp

Freshly ground black pepper 1 tsp

- Heat ghee in a wok and sauté onions, cloves and cardamoms until onions are soft.

- Add combined spices and chicken. Fry over medium heat until fragrant.

- Add in tomato purée, evaporated milk and a little water. Cook until the gravy thickens slightly.

- Season with salt and sugar. Add in yoghurt, coriander leaves and green chillies. Cook until the gravy is thick. Garnish as desired and erve hot with rice.

DEVIL'S CHICKEN
AYAM DEBAL

Cooking oil 2 Tbsp

Mustard seeds 1 Tbsp

Onion 1, large, peeled and sliced

Shallots 10, peeled and finely minced

Cumin powder 1 Tbsp

Dried chillies 20, soaked, seeded, drained and finely minced

Turmeric 1 thumb-size knob, peeled and finely minced

Garlic 6 cloves, peeled and finely minced

Ginger 2.5-cm (1-in) knob, peeled and finely minced

Chicken 1, about 1 kg (2 lb 3 oz), cleaned and cut into bite-size pieces

Curry leaves 2 sprigs

White vinegar to taste

Salt to taste

- Heat oil in a deep pan and fry mustard seeds. When seeds crackle, add onions and fry until browned.

- Add shallots, cumin, chillies, turmeric, garlic and ginger and fry for a few minutes.

- Add chicken and curry leaves and stir well, frying until chicken is well coated with the spices. Reduce heat and simmer until chicken is tender.

- Add vinegar and salt to taste and cook for a few more minutes over low heat before serving.

DUCK EGGS IN DHAL GRAVY
TELUR ITIK BERSAMA KUAH DHAL

Dried chillies 20, soaked, seeded and drained

Shallots 6, peeled

Turmeric 3-cm (1½-in) knob, peeled

Dried anchovies (*ikan bilis*) 15 g (½ oz)

Dried sour fruit (*asam gelugor*) 3 pieces

Coconut milk 250 ml (8 fl oz / 1 cup), extracted from 1 grated coconut and 250 ml (8 fl oz / 1 cup) water

Dhal 100 g (3½ oz)

Store-bought coconut cream 500 ml (16 fl oz / 2 cups)

Salt to taste

Duck eggs 3–4, hard-boiled and shelled

- Boil a pot of water and cook dhal for about 30 minutes until soft. Set aside.

- Pound or grind dried chillies, shallots, turmeric and dried anchovies into a fine paste.

- Put the paste into a pot together with dried sour fruit pieces and coconut milk. Bring to the boil.

- Add in cooked dhal, coconut cream and salt. Add duck eggs to the sauce and cook for 5 minutes. Garnish as desired and serve warm with rice.

FISH & SEAFOOD

SEA BASS IN TANGY GRAVY
SIAKAP ASAM TUMIS

Vegetable oil 4 Tbsp

Tamarind juice 125 ml (4 fl oz / ½ cup), made from 1 Tbsp tamarind pulp mixed with 125 ml (4 fl oz / ½ cup) water and strained

Water 250 ml (8 fl oz / 1 cup)

Ladies fingers (okra) 6, stemmed

Sea bass 1, large, cut into 4 pieces

Laksa **leaves** 1 bunch

Salt to taste

Sugar to taste

Spice paste

Ground chilli paste 4 Tbsp

Dried prawn (shrimp) paste (*belacan*) 1 Tbsp

Shallots 6, peeled

Turmeric 1-cm (½-in) knob, peeled

Garlic 3 cloves, peeled

Kaffir lime leaf 1, central stem removed

- Combine ingredients for spice paste in a food processor and blend until smooth. Heat oil in a wok and sauté spice paste until fragrant. Add the tamarind juice, water and Ladies fingers and simmer for 10 minutes.

- Add sea bass and *laksa* leaves. Simmer for another 5 minutes. Season with salt and sugar. Garnish as desired and serve warm with rice.

MY EX-WIFE'S CATFISH IN BIRD'S EYE CHILLI GRAVY
IKAN SEMBILANG LEMAK CILI API JANDAKU

My ex-wife makes the best catfish in bird's eye chilli gravy that I have ever tasted. Over the years I have not been able to acquire her skills, despite my vast culinary knowledge. Although people who come from Negeri Sembilan swear that their recipe is the best, my ex-wife says that she is from Malacca and her recipe is better! So test it out. This dish must be cooked in a *belanga* (clay pot).

Catfish 1, about 1 kg (2 lb 3 oz), cut into 8 pieces, cleaned and barbecued over glowing charcoal

Limes 3, juice extracted + more to taste

Coconut milk 500 ml (16 fl oz / 2 cups), extracted from 1½ grated coconuts 500 ml (16 fl oz / 2 cups) water, and then squeezed again for 750 ml (24 fl oz / 3 cups) second-squeeze coconut milk using 750 ml (24 fl oz / 3 cups) water

Salt to taste

Spice paste

Bird's eye chillies (*cili padi*) 30, seeded

Turmeric 2-cm (1-in) knob, peeled

- Combine ingredients for spice paste in a mortar and pound until smooth. In a clay pot, combine catfish with lime juice and finely pounded paste. Cook over low heat for 10 minutes.

- Add the second-squeeze coconut milk and simmer for 10 minutes.

- Add the first-squeeze coconut milk and simmer for 5 minutes.

- Season with salt and more lime juice if desired. Serve warm with rice.

PORTUGUESE BAKED FISH
IKAN BAKAR PORTUGIS

Cooking oil 4 Tbsp

Lime 1/2, juice extracted

Dark soy sauce 1/2 Tbsp

Salt to taste

Sugar to taste

Pomfret 1, about 600 g (1 lb 5 oz)

Banana leaf 1 piece

Spice paste

Red chillies 4, seeded

Candlenuts 4

Shallots 8, peeled

Lemongrass 1 stalk, finely sliced

Dried prawn (shrimp) paste (*belacan*) 1/2 tsp

Chilli powder 1 Tbsp

Kaffir lime leaves 2

- Combine ingredients for spice paste in a food processor and blend until smooth. Heat oil in a wok and sauté the spice paste over low heat until fragrant. Add lime juice, soy sauce, salt and sugar.

- Spread cooked paste over fish and wrap fish in a piece of banana leaf.

- Bake in a preheated oven for 20 minutes at 180°C (350°F) or grill over glowing charcoal. Garnish as desired and serve warm with rice.

FISH IN PRESERVED SOY BEANS
IKAN KURAU BERKUAH TAU CHEO

Threadfin 3, large

Salt to taste

Freshly ground black pepper to taste

Cooking oil for shallow-frying + 4 Tbsp

Garlic 3 cloves, peeled and finely chopped

Ginger 1-cm (1/2-in) knob, peeled and
   sliced

Tomatoes 3, cut into small cubes

Preserved soy beans (*tau cheo*) 2 Tbsp,
   washed under running water

Spring onions (scallions) 3, chopped

Sauce

Oyster sauce 2 tsp

Sugar 1/4 tsp

Sesame oil 1 tsp

Salt a pinch

Corn flour (cornstarch) 2 Tbsp

Chicken stock (see Note on page 70)
   4 Tbsp

- Rub the fish with salt and pepper and shallow-fry in hot oil until crisp.
  Drain and set aside.

- In a clean wok, heat 4 Tbsp oil and sauté the garlic and ginger.

- Add tomatoes and preserved soy beans and cook until the tomatoes
  are soft.

- Combine ingredients for sauce in a bowl and stir to mix well. Add the
  sauce ingredients to the wok and bring to a simmer.

- Add spring onions and fish and stir until the sauce is cooked. Garnish
  as desired and serve warm with rice.

HARD-TAILED SCAD STUFFED WITH CHILLI
CENCARU SUMBAT CILI

Hard-tailed scad 3, cleaned and rubbed
with turmeric powder

Red chillies 10, seeded and finely minced

Shallots 8, peeled and finely minced

Dried prawn (shrimp) paste (*belacan*) 1 tsp

Salt to taste

Sugar to taste

Tamarind juice 1 Tbsp, made from 1 tsp
tamarind pulp mixed with 1 Tbsp water
or to taste and strained

Cooking oil for deep-frying

- Make a deep slit along one side of fish. Set aside.
- Mix chillies, shallots, prawn paste, salt, sugar and tamarind juice together to form a thick paste.
- Stuff the paste into fish.
- Heat the oil in a wok and deep-fry until cooked. Serve immediately.

SULTAN FISH IN TOM YAM GRAVY
JELAWAT MASAK TOM YAM

Sultan fish or *jelawat* is a freshwater fish popular with Malaysians.

Cooking oil 6 Tbsp

Aubergines (eggplants/brinjal) 2, quartered

Ladies fingers (okra) 4, stemmed

***Tom yam* paste** 2 Tbsp

Water 125 ml (4 fl oz / 1/2 cup)

Coconut milk 125 ml (4 fl oz / 1/2 cup), extracted from 1/2 grated coconut and 125 ml (4 fl oz / 1/2 cup) water

Tomato 1, halved

Bird's eye chillies (*cili padi*) 5, seeded

Torch ginger bud 1, halved lengthways

Sultan fish 1, about 500 g (1 lb 1 1/2 oz)

Lime 1, juice extracted

Kaffir lime leaves 2, finely sliced

- Heat 4 Tbsp oil in a wok and stir-fry the aubergines and ladies fingers. Drain and set aside.

- In a clean wok, heat the remaining oil and sauté *tom yam* paste until fragrant. Pour in water and coconut milk and bring to a simmer.

- Add fried eggplants and ladies fingers, tomato, chillies and torch ginger bud. Simmer for 5 minutes.

- Add the fish and simmer for 10 minutes before adding lime juice and kaffir lime leaves. Serve immediately.

SPICY AND SOUR FISH
ASAM PEDAS

Vegetable oil 125 ml (4 fl oz / ¹/₂ cup)

Tamarind juice 125 ml (4 fl oz / ¹/₂ cup), made from 2 Tbsp tamarind pulp mixed with 125 ml (4 fl oz / ¹/₂ cup) water and strained

Pineapple 1 slice, cut into chunks

Tomatoes 2, cut into wedges

Water 4 Tbsp

Salt to taste

Sugar to taste

Torch ginger bud 1, quartered

Bird's eye chillies (*cili padi*) 4, seeded

Red chillies 2, seeded and sliced lengthwise

Laksa **leaves** 10

Sea bass 1, about 800 g (1³/₄ lb), cleaned and gutted

Lime juice 2 Tbsp

Kaffir lime leaves 2, finely sliced

Coriander leaves (cilantro) 2 stalks, shredded

Spice paste

Red chillies 8, seeded

Bird's eye chillies (*cili padi*) 3, seeded

Candlenuts 6

Turmeric 2-cm (1-in) knob, peeled

Dried prawn (shrimp) paste (*belacan*) 2 tsp

Coriander leaves (cilantro) 3 stalks

Kaffir lime leaves 2

Shallots 8, peeled

Garlic 3 cloves, peeled

Young ginger 1-cm (¹/₂-in) knob, peeled

- Combine ingredients for spice paste in a food processor and blend until smooth.

- Heat oil in a wok and sauté the spice paste until fragrant.

- Add tamarind juice, pineapple, tomatoes and water. Bring to the boil. Simmer until sauce thickens. Season with salt and sugar. Then, put in the torch ginger bud, bird's eye chillies, red chillies and *laksa* leaves.

- Place the fish on a dish. Pour the sauce over and steam for 15–20 minutes until fish is cooked.

- Drizzle lime juice over fish and garnish with kaffir lime leaves and coriander leaves. Serve immediately.

STEAMED FISH
IKAN KUKUS

Snapper or sea bass 1, about 500 g
  (1 lb 1½ oz)

Fish sauce 2 tsp

Corn flour (cornstarch) ½ tsp

Torch ginger bud 1, finely sliced

Lemongrass 1 stalk, finely sliced

Red chillies 5, seeded and finely sliced

Kaffir lime leaves 2, central stems
  removed and finely sliced

Young ginger 1-cm (½-in) knob, peeled
  and finely sliced

Garlic 2 cloves, peeled and finely sliced

Coriander leaves (cilantro) 1 sprig,
  chopped

Spring onion (scallion) 1, chopped

Seasoning

Salt to taste

Sugar 1½ Tbsp

Kalamansi lime juice 3–3½ Tbsp

Anchovy (*ikan bilis*) stock granules ½ tsp

Corn flour (cornstarch) ¾ tsp

- Combine fish, fish sauce and corn flour in a greased serving dish and set aside to marinate for 10 minutes.

- Combine the torch ginger bud, lemongrass, chillies, kaffir lime leaves, young ginger, garlic and seasoning ingredients. Pour over the fish and steam over rapidly boiling water for 5 minutes.

- Garnish with coriander leaves and spring onion. Serve immediately.

FRIED CHILLI CATFISH
IKAN KELI GORENG CILI

Catfish 1, about 1 kg (2 lb 3 oz), gutted, marinated with the juice of 3 limes for 1 hour and cleaned

Turmeric powder 1/4 tsp

Salt to taste

Vegetable oil 85 ml (2 1/2 fl oz / 1/3 cup)

Tamarind juice 2 Tbsp, made from 1 Tbsp tamarind pulp mixed with 2 Tbsp water and strained

Sugar to taste

Spice paste

Red chillies 7, seeded

Bird's eye chillies (*cili padi*) 15, seeded

Shallots 10, peeled

- Season fish with turmeric powder and salt. Heat oil in wok and deep-fry the fish until crisp. Remove and drain.

- Combine ingredients for spice paste in a food processor and blend until smooth. Fry the spice in the remaining oil until fragrant.

- Add fried fish, tamarind juice, sugar and salt. Stir well to combine.

- Remove from heat and garnish as desired. Serve immediately.

FISH CURRY
KARI IKAN

Vegetable oil 6 Tbsp

Mustard seeds 1 Tbsp

Fenugreek ½ tsp

Curry leaves 3 sprigs

Fish curry powder 6 Tbsp, mixed with 8 Tbsp water to form a smooth paste

Coconut milk 500 ml (16 fl oz / 2 cups), extracted from 1 grated coconut and 500 ml (16 fl oz / 2 cups) water

Tamarind juice 2 Tbsp, made from 1 Tbsp tamarind pulp mixed with 2 Tbsp water and strained

Japanese aubergines (*nasu***/eggplants)** 2, cut into 2-cm (1-in) lengths

Spanish mackerel 600 g (1 lb 5⅓ oz), cleaned and cut into pieces

Red chilli 1, seeded and halved lengthwise

Green chilli 1, seeded and halved lengthwise

Water (optional) 250 ml (8 fl oz / 1 cup)

Salt to taste

Spice paste

Shallots 10, peeled

Garlic 4 cloves, peeled

Ginger 2-cm (1-in) knob, peeled

- Combine ingredients for spice paste in a food processor and blend until smooth. Heat oil in a wok and fry the spice paste, mustard seeds, fenugreek and curry leaves until fragrant.

- Add the fish curry paste and fry until fragrant.

- Add coconut milk, tamarind juice and eggplants and simmer gently for 20 minutes until the eggplants are cooked.

- Add the fish and chillies. Add water if you want to dilute the curry. Simmer for 12 minutes. Season with salt and serve warm with rice.

TALANG FISH IN COCONUT GRAVY
GULAI LEMAK IKAN TALANG MASIN BERSAMA NANAS

Bird's eye chillies (*cili padi*) 25, seeded and finely minced

Turmeric 3-cm (1$^1/_2$-in) knob, peeled and finely minced

Coconut milk 500 ml (16 fl oz / 2 cups), extracted from 1 grated coconut and 500 ml (16 fl oz / 2 cups) water

Pineapple $^1/_2$, peeled and cubed

Lemongrass 1 stalk, bruised

Dried sour fruit (*asam gelugor*) 2 pieces

Salted *talang* fish 500 g (1 lb 1$^1/_2$ oz), cubed and soaked overnight

Sugar to taste

- Heat a pot and put in all the ingredients. Boil for 15 minutes.
- Season with sugar to taste. Serve immediately.

SILVER CATFISH IN FERMENTED DURIAN GRAVY
IKAN PATIN MASAK GULAI TEMPOYAK

Fermented durian 8 Tbsp

Lemongrass 2 stalks, bruised

Water 200 ml (6³/₄ fl oz)

Dried sour fruit (*asam gelugor*) 2 pieces

Silver catfish 1, about 500 g (1 lb 1¹/₂ oz), cleaned, gutted and cut into 3 pieces

Salt to taste

Sugar to taste

Pounded ingredients

Red bird's eye chillies (*cili padi*) 30, seeded

Turmeric 3-cm (1¹/₂-in) knob, peeled

- Combine fermented durian, lemongrass, water, dried sour fruit and ponded ingredients in a pot and bring to the boil. Simmer for 5 minutes.

- Put in the fish and cook for a further 10 minutes until fish is done. Season with salt and sugar. Serve warm with rice.

MACKEREL IN SPICY AND SOUR GRAVY
GERANG ASAM

Vegetable oil 125 ml (4 fl oz / ¹/₂ cup)

Torch ginger bud 1, halved lengthwise

Kaffir lime leaves 3

Tamarind juice 250 ml (8 fl oz / 1 cup), made from 3 Tbsp tamarind pulp mixed with 250 ml (8 fl oz / 1 cup) water and strained

Ladies fingers (okra) 8, trimmed

Spotted Spanish mackerel 4 steaks, each about 125 g (4¹/₂ oz), cleaned

Salt to taste

Sugar to taste

Spice paste

Dried chillies 25, soaked in water, seeded and drained

Dried prawn (shrimp) paste (*belacan*) 2-cm (1-in)

Turmeric 2-cm (1-in) knob, peeled

Lemongrass 2 stalks, sliced

Galangal 1-cm (¹/₂-in) knob, peeled

Candlenuts 5

Garlic 2 cloves, peeled

Shallots 10, peeled

- Combine ingredients for spice paste in a food processor and blend until smooth.

- Heat oil in a wok and sauté the spice paste over medium heat until fragrant.

- Add torch ginger bud and kaffir lime leaves. Allow to simmer for a few minutes.

- Pour in tamarind juice. Bring to the boil before adding ladies fingers and fish. Simmer for a further 3 minutes.

- Season with salt and sugar. Serve hot.

SPANISH MACKEREL IN SOY SAUCE
IKAN TENGGIRI MASAK KICAP

Vegetable oil 2 Tbsp

Garlic 2 cloves, peeled and sliced

Ginger 2-cm (1-in) knob, peeled and sliced

White vinegar 1 tsp

Light soy sauce 250 ml (8 fl oz / 1 cup)

Water 2 Tbsp

Sugar to taste

Spanish mackerel 1 steak, about 200 g (7 oz), marinated with turmeric powder and deep-fried until golden brown

Red chilli 1, seeded and halved lengthwise

Green chilli 1, seeded and halved lengthwise

Onion $1/2$, peeled and sliced into rings

- Heat oil in a wok and sauté garlic and ginger until golden brown.
- Add the rest of the ingredients and bring to the boil.
- Allow to simmer over low heat until sauce thickens slightly. Serve hot.

SKATE IN HOT GRAVY
IKAN PARI KUAH LADA

Vegetable oil 3 Tbsp

Grated coconut 6 Tbsp, dry-fried until golden

Aubergine (eggplant/brinjal) 1, cut into small pieces

Tamarind juice 375 ml (12 fl oz / 1½ cup), made from 1 Tbsp tamarind pulp mixed with 375 ml (12 fl oz / 1½ cup) water and strained

Skate 500 g (1 lb 1½ oz), cleaned and cut into pieces

Salt to taste

Sugar to taste

Spice paste

Onions 4, peeled

Garlic 2 cloves, peeled

Cumin powder 1 tsp

Coriander powder 1 tsp

Ground chilli paste 2 Tbsp

Black peppercorns 1 tsp

- Combine ingredients for spice paste in a food processor and blend until smooth. Heat oil in a wok and fry the spice paste until fragrant.

- Add grated coconut and aubergine and stir-fry for a few minutes.

- Add tamarind juice and simmer for a few minutes.

- Add the skate and cook for 10–15 minutes. Season with salt and sugar. Garnish as desired and serve warm with rice.

BLACK POMFRET COOKED WITH KALAMANSI LIMES
IKAN BAWAL KASTURI

Cooking oil for deep-frying + 2 Tbsp

Black pomfret 1, about 500 g
(1 lb 1½ oz), cleaned and
seasoned with turmeric powder

Coconut milk 500 ml (16 fl oz /
2 cups), extracted from
1 grated coconut and 500 ml
(16 fl oz / 2 cups) water

Lemongrass 2 stalks, bruised

Sour star fruit (*belimbing buluh*) 4,
halved

Kaffir lime leaves 3

Kalamansi limes 4, juice extracted

Sugar to taste

Spice paste

Shallots 6, peeled

Red chillies 8, seeded

Bird's eye chillies (*cili padi*) 4, seeded

Turmeric 3-cm (1½-in) knob, peeled

Ginger 1-cm (½-in) knob, peeled

Garlic 2 cloves, peeled

- Combine ingredients for spice paste in a food processor and
  blend until smooth. Set aside.

- Heat oil for deep-frying in a wok and fry the fish. Remove
  and set aside.

- Heat 2 Tbsp oil in the wok and sauté the spice paste
  until fragrant.

- Add coconut milk, lemongrass, sour star fruit, kaffir lime
  leaves and lime juice. Add sugar to taste. Garnish as
  desired and serve immediately with rice.

SWEET AND SOUR FISH
IKAN MASAK MASAM MANIS

Sea bass 1, about 400 g (14 oz), sliced open lengthwise

Salt to taste

Corn flour (cornstarch) ½ tsp + more to thicken gravy

Cooking oil for deep-frying

Garlic 2 cloves, peeled and chopped

Onion 1, large, peeled and sliced

Pineapple 1 slice, diced

Red capsicum (bell pepper) ½, cored and sliced

Green capsicum (bell pepper) ½, cored and sliced

Sugar to taste

Sauce

Canned tomato sauce 2 Tbsp

Plum sauce 2 Tbsp

Oyster sauce 1 tsp

White vinegar 1 tsp

Water 125 ml (4 fl oz / ½ cup)

Corn flour (cornstarch) ½ tsp mixed with ½ tsp water

Salt to taste

Sugar to taste

- Season fish with salt and corn flour. Heat oil in a wok and deep-fry fish until golden brown and crisp. Remove from oil and set aside.

- Remove some oil leaving 2–3 Tbsp in the wok and fry garlic and onion until soft.

- Combine all ingredients for sauce in a bowl and stir to mix well. Add the sauce into the wok and bring to the boil. Add the pineapple and simmer for about 2 minutes.

- Add capsicums, sugar and salt to taste.

- Add more corn flour and stir to thicken gravy slightly. Pour gravy over fish and serve immediately.

ANCHOVIES WITH SOY SAUCE
IKAN BILIS GORENG KICAP

Cooking oil 2 Tbsp

Anchovies (*ikan bilis*) 300 g (10½ oz)

Garlic 3, peeled and sliced

Red chilli 1, seeded and sliced

Green chilli 1, seeded and sliced

Onion 1, peeled and sliced

Dark soy sauce 4 Tbsp

Kalamansi lime 1, juice extracted

Sugar 1 tsp

- Heat oil in a wok and fry anchovies until golden brown.
- Add garlic, chillies, onion, soy sauce and lime juice and stir-fry until well mixed.
- Finally, add in the sugar and mix well. Serve immediately.

STUFFED CHILLI
SOLOK LADA

Red chillies 10, seeded

Coconut milk 300 ml (10 fl oz / 1¼ cups), extracted from 1½ coconuts and 300 ml (10 fl oz / 1¼ cups) water

Water 125 ml (4 fl oz / ½ cup)

Lemongrass 1 stalk, bruised

Galangal 1-cm (½-in) knob, bruised

Salt to taste

Sugar to taste

Ground ingredients

Coconut ½, grated

Spanish mackerel flesh 400 g (14 oz)

Dried prawns (shrimps) 2 Tbsp, finely pounded

Shallots 6, peeled

Ginger 2-cm (1-in) knob, peeled and sliced

- Put ground ingredients in a bowl and season with salt and sugar to taste. Mix well.

- Stuff chillies with the ground ingredients. Place stuffed chillies into a pot.

- Add coconut milk, lemongrass and galangal. Cook slowly over low heat until the gravy thickens. Serve warm.

PRAWN MASALA
UDANG MASALA

Prawns (shrimps) 900 g (2 lb), cleaned and shelled with tails intact

Salt 1/2 Tbsp + more to taste

Turmeric powder 2 Tbsp

Garlic 5 cloves, peeled and finely minced

Shallots 5, peeled and finely minced + 5, peeled and thinly sliced

Ginger 2.5-cm (1-in) knob, peeled and finely minced

Cooking oil for shallow-frying

Chilli powder 1 Tbsp

Sweet cumin powder 2 Tbsp

Ground white pepper 1 Tbsp

Tomato sauce 2 Tbsp

Grated coconut flesh 3 Tbsp

Tamarind juice 125 ml (4 fl oz / 1/2 cup), made from 1 Tbsp tamarind pulp mixed with 125 ml (4 fl oz / 1/2 cup) water and strained

Sugar to taste

Fried shallots for garnishing

- Season prawns with 1/2 Tbsp salt, turmeric powder, garlic, finely minced shallots and ginger for 30 minutes.

- Heat oil in a wok and brown the remaining shallots. Add chilli powder, cumin powder and pepper and fry until fragrant.

- Add tomato sauce, prawns, coconut, tamarind juice, salt and sugar. Cook for another 5 minutes. Garnish with fried shallots and serve immediately with rice.

PRAWNS WITH PINEAPPLE IN SPICY GRAVY
KARI UDANG BERNANAS THAI

Vegetable oil 85 ml (2½ fl oz / ⅓ cup)

Store-bought cream 800 ml (27 fl oz)

Palm sugar (*gula melaka*) 4 Tbsp, grated

Pineapple ½, peeled and diced

Freshwater prawns (shrimps) 500 g
(1 lb 1½ oz), cleaned and feelers
trimmed

Thai basil leaves 40

Lime 1, juice extracted

Salt to taste

Sugar 4 tsp

Spice paste

Red chillies 8, seeded

Turmeric 1-cm (½-in) knob, peeled

Candlenuts 4

Garlic 2 cloves, peeled

Shallots 8, peeled

Coriander root 4

Dried prawn (shrimp) paste (*belacan*) 1 tsp

Coriander powder 2 tsp

Galangal 2-cm (1-in) knob, peeled

Lemongrass 3 stalks, bruised

- Combine ingredients for spice paste in a food processor and blend until smooth.

- Heat oil in wok and fry the spice paste over low heat until the oil surfaces.

- Add coconut cream, palm sugar and pineapple. Bring to the boil and simmer for 5 minutes.

- Put in the prawns, basil leaves, lime juice, salt and sugar to taste. Cook for a further 5 minutes. Serve warm with rice.

FRESHWATER PRAWN RENDANG
RENDANG UDANG GALAH

Cooking oil 4 Tbsp

Freshwater prawns (shrimps) 1 kg
  (2 lb 3 oz), cleaned and feelers trimmed

Shallots 500 g (1 lb 1½ oz), peeled and
  thinly sliced

Ginger 4-cm (2-in) knob, peeled and
  thinly sliced

Lemongrass 4 stalks, finely sliced

Turmeric leaf 1, finely sliced + more
  for garnishing

Dried chillies 20, soaked, seeded, drained
  and coarsely pounded

Coconut milk 750 ml (24 fl oz / 3 cups),
  extracted from 2 coconuts and 750 ml
  (24 fl oz / 3 cups) water

Salt to taste

Sugar to taste

- Heat oil in a wok and put in all the ingredients.

- Cook over medium heat until it comes to the boil. Turn down the heat
  and continue to simmer until gravy thickens.

- Garnish with finely sliced turmeric leaf and serve immediately with rice.

PRAWN AND STINK BEAN SAMBAL
SAMBAL UDANG PETAI

Cooking oil 85 ml (2¹/₂ fl oz / ¹/₃ cup)

Tamarind juice 50 ml (1³/₄ fl oz), made from 1 Tbsp tamarind pulp mixed with 2 Tbsp water and strained

Stink beans 40, peeled

Prawns (shrimps) 500 g (1 lb 1¹/₂ oz), cleaned and shelled leaving tails intact

Salt to taste

Sugar 6 Tbsp

Spice paste

Shallots 10, peeled

Dried chillies 30, soaked, seeded and drained

Dried prawn (shrimp) paste (*belacan*) 1 Tbsp

- Combine ingredients for spice paste in a food processor and blend until smooth.

- Heat oil in a wok and stir-fry the spice paste until fragrant and the oil surfaces.

- Add tamarind juice, stink beans and prawns. Stir-fry for 2 minutes, then season with salt and sugar. Serve immediately.

PRAWNS WITH SAMBAL BELACAN
UDANG DENGAN SAMBAL BELACAN

Prawns (shrimps) 6, large, cleaned and feelers trimmed

Corn flour (cornstarch) as needed

Cooking oil 3 Tbsp

Salt to taste

Thick tamarind paste 2 tsp

Sugar 1 tsp or to taste

Spice paste

Red chillies 8, seeded

Bird's eye chillies (*cili padi*) 3, seeded

Dried prawn (shrimp) paste (*belacan*) 1 Tbsp

Garlic 1 clove, peeled

Cooking oil 3 Tbsp

- Lightly sprinkle prawns with corn flour.

- Heat oil in a wok and fry the prawns on high heat. Add a bit of salt.

- Remove prawns from the wok and set aside.

- Combine ingredients for spice paste in a food processor and blend until smooth. Fry the spice paste over low heat until fragrant.

- Add in the prawns, tamarind paste and sugar to taste.

- Fry to mix evenly and remove from wok. Serve hot with rice.

STIR-FRIED PRAWNS WITH PANDAN LEAVES
UDANG GORENG BERSAMA DAUN PANDAN

Prawns (shrimps) 500 g (1 lb 1¹/₂ oz), cleaned and feelers trimmed

Corn flour (cornstarch) 1 Tbsp

Egg yolk 1, beaten

Oyster sauce ¹/₂ tsp

Cooking oil for deep-frying

Tomato 1, quartered

Golden raisins 4 Tbsp

White sesame seeds to garnish, toasted

Sauce

Vegetable oil 3 Tbsp

Shallots 9, peeled and finely chopped

Garlic 3 cloves, peeled and finely chopped

Ginger 2-cm (1-in) knob, peeled and finely sliced

Ground chilli paste 2 tsp

Pandan leaves 2, tied into a knot

Lemongrass 2 stalks, bruised

Honey 2 Tbsp

Kalamansi lime ¹/₂, juice extracted

Salt to taste

- Combine prawns, corn flour, egg yolk and oyster sauce in a bowl and mix well. Heat oil in a wok and deep-fry the prawns until golden. Set aside.

- Prepare sauce. Heat oil in a wok and stir-fry shallots, garlic, ginger and ground chilli paste until fragrant. Add the pandan leaves, lemongrass, honey and lime juice. Season with salt.

- Stir in the fried prawns and tomato. Garnish with raisins and sesame seeds. Serve immediately with rice.

PRAWNS AND PUMPKIN IN COCONUT GRAVY
GULAI UDANG DAN LABU PEDAS

Pumpkin 300 g (10½ oz), peeled and cut into large chunks

Coconut milk 500 ml (16 fl oz / 2 cups), extracted from 1 grated coconut and 500 ml (16 fl oz / 2 cups) water

Turmeric leaf 1, finely sliced

Prawns (shrimps) 200 g (7 oz), cleaned and shelled

Sugar to taste

Salt to taste

Pounded ingredients

Dried prawns (shrimps) 2 Tbsp, soaked and drained

Shallots 3, peeled

Garlic 1 clove, peeled

- Put the pounded ingredients, pumpkin and coconut milk into a pot. Bring to the boil and simmer until the pumpkin is soft.

- Add the turmeric leaf and prawns and cook for a further 3 minutes.

- Season with sugar and salt. Garnish as desired and serve warm with rice.

KALIO PRAWNS
KALIO UDANG

Vegetable oil 4 Tbsp

Coconut milk 500 ml (16 fl oz / 2 cups), extracted from 1 grated coconut and 500 ml (16 fl oz / 2 cups) water

Prawns (shrimps) 1 kg (2 lb 3 oz), cleaned and feelers trimmed

Dried sour fruit (*asam gelugor*) 4 pieces

Salt to taste

Sugar to taste

Green mango 1, peeled and coarsely shredded

Finely chopped *laksa* leaves 4 Tbsp

Turmeric leaf 1, finely sliced

Spice paste

Red chillies 10, seeded

Bird's eye chillies (*cili padi*) 8, seeded

Candlenuts 6

Lemongrass 3 stalks

Galangal 2-cm (1-in) knob, peeled

Kaffir lime leaves 2

Coriander leaves (cilantro) 3 sprigs

- Combine ingredients for spice paste in a food processor and blend until smooth.

- Heat oil in a wok over medium heat and sauté the spice paste until fragrant.

- Pour in the coconut milk. Add the prawns, dried sour fruit, salt and sugar. Bring to the boil and simmer for 10 minutes until the prawns are cooked.

- Put in the mango, *laksa* leaves and turmeric leaf.

- Cook for another 15 minutes until sauce thickens. Serve warm with rice.

CHILLI CRAB
KETAM BERCILI

Cooking oil for deep-frying + 2 Tbsp

Crabs 3, about 1.2–1.5 kg (2 lb 10 oz–3 lb 4¹/₂ oz), cleaned and halved

Corn flour (cornstarch) 2 Tbsp, mixed with 4 Tbsp water

Egg 1, beaten

Spring onions (scallions) 2, chopped

Coriander leaves (cilantro) a few sprigs

Spice paste

Chilli powder 1¹/₂ Tbsp

Red chillies 6, seeded

Garlic 6 cloves, peeled

Shallots 100 g (3¹/₂ oz), peeled

Ginger 1-cm (¹/₂-in) knob, peeled

Sauce

Chilli sauce 3 Tbsp

Sugar 2 Tbsp

White vinegar 2 Tbsp

Canned tomato sauce 250 ml (8 fl oz / 1 cup)

Salt to taste

- Heat oil in a wok and deep-fry the crabs until golden. Drain and set aside.

- Combine ingredients for spice paste in a food processor and blend until smooth. Heat 2 Tbsp oil in a wok and sauté the spice paste until fragrant.

- Meanwhile, combine ingredients for the sauce in a bowl and stir to mix well. Add to the wok and bring the mixture to a boil. Cover and simmer for about 10 minutes.

- Gradually add the corn flour mixture and stir well. Add the beaten egg. Gently stir in the fried crabs and simmer until the sauce is cooked.

- Garnish with spring onions and coriander leaves. Serve immediately with rice.

CRAB AND PINEAPPLE CURRY
GULAI LEMAK KETAM BERSAMA NANAS

Bird's eye chillies (*cili padi*) 30, seeded

Turmeric 3-cm (1^1/$_2$-in) knob, peeled

Coconut milk 1 litre (32 fl oz / 4 cups), extracted from 1^1/$_2$ grated coconuts and 1 litre (32 fl oz / 4 cups) water

Pineapple ^{1}/$_2$, peeled and sliced

Dried sour fruit (*asam gelugor*) 3 pieces

Sugar to taste

Salt to taste

Turmeric leaves 2, shredded

Crabs 3, about 1 kg (2 lb 3 oz), cleaned and halved

- Pound the bird's eye chillies and turmeric to a paste. Put paste in a pot together with coconut milk and pineapple. Bring to the boil and simmer for 15 minutes.

- Add dried sour fruit, sugar, salt and turmeric leaves.

- When gravy comes to the boil, put in the crabs and cook for a further 5 minutes until crabs are done. Season with more salt and sugar to taste. Serve warm with rice.

KAM HEONG CRAB

KETAM KAM HEONG

Cooking oil for deep-frying + 3 Tbsp

Crabs 3, about 1 kg (2 lb 3 oz), cleaned and halved

Garlic 5 cloves, peeled and minced

Dried prawns (shrimps) 2 Tbsp

Curry powder 2 Tbsp

Curry leaves 3

Bird's eye chillies (*cili padi*) 6, seeded and sliced

Oyster sauce 2 Tbsp

Freshly ground black pepper 1 tsp

Salt to taste

Sugar to taste

- Heat oil for deep-frying in a wok and fry the crabs for about 5 minutes on each side until cooked. Set aside.

- In a clean wok, heat 3 Tbsp oil and stir-fry the garlic until fragrant. Add dried prawns and stir until prawns are cooked. Add curry powder, curry leaves and bird's eye chillies and stir-fry for a few more minutes. Add oyster sauce and pepper and mix well.

- Put in the crabs and mix until well coated with the sauce. Season with salt and sugar. Serve immediately.

SINGGANG CRAB WITH PINEAPPLE
KETAM MASAK SINGGANG BERSAMA NANAS

Water 250 ml (8 fl oz / 1 cup)

Turmeric 2-cm (1-in) knob, peeled and sliced

Lemongrass 2 stalks, bruised

Dried sour fruit (*asam gelugor*) 2 pieces

Ginger 2.5 cm (1-in) knob, peeled and sliced

Dried prawns (shrimps) 2 Tbsp, washed and ground

Green chilli ¹/₂, seeded and cut in half lengthwise

Red chilli ¹/₂, seeded and cut in half lengthwise

Pineapple 1, peeled and thinly sliced

Crabs 3, about 1 kg (2 lb 3 oz), cleaned and halved

Salt to taste

Sugar 2 tsp

- Heat water in a saucepan. Add turmeric, lemongrass, garlic, dried sour fruit, ginger and dried prawns and bring to the boil.
- Put in the green and red chillies. Add the pineapple.
- Put in the crabs and stir until crabs are cooked through. Add salt and sugar to taste. Serve immediately.

STIR-FRIED SQUID IN BLACK INK
SOTONG MASAK HITAM

Vegetable oil 4 Tbsp

Shallots 4, peeled and thinly sliced

Garlic 3 cloves, peeled and thinly sliced

Lemongrass 3 stalks, finely sliced

Squid 800 g (1¾ lb), cleaned and cut into rings, ink reserved

Onion 1, peeled and thinly sliced

Red chillies 2, seeded and sliced lengthwise

Tamarind juice 75 ml (2½ fl oz / ⅓ cup), made from 1 Tbsp tamarind pulp mixed with 75 ml (2½ fl oz / ⅓ cup) water and strained

Salt to taste

Sugar to taste

- Heat oil in a wok and stir-fry shallots and garlic until crisp and golden brown.

- Add the lemongrass and sauté for a couple of minutes.

- Put in the squid, squid ink, onion, chillies, tamarind juice, salt and sugar. Stir well and cook for another 5 minutes. Garnish as desired and serve immediately with rice.

NYONYA SQUID SAMBAL
SOTONG GORENG NYONYA

Cooking oil 85 ml (2¹/₂ fl oz / ¹/₃ cup)

Squid 500 g (1 lb 1¹/₂ oz), cleaned and sliced

Sour star fruit (*belimbing buluh*) 8, halved

Kalamansi limes 4, juice extracted

Tomato sauce 125 ml (4 fl oz / ¹/₂ cup)

Sugar to taste

Mint leaves 30 + more for garnishing

Salt to taste

Spice paste

Red chillies 8, seeded

Bird's eye chillies (*cili padi*) 3, seeded

Onions 4, peeled

Garlic 1 clove, peeled

Dried prawns (shrimp) paste (*belacan*) 1 tsp

Turmeric 1-cm (¹/₂-in) knob, peeled

Ginger 1-cm (¹/₂-in) knob, peeled

Kaffir lime leaves 2

Lemongrass 2 stalks

Candlenuts 5

- Combine ingredients for spice paste in a food processor and blend until smooth.

- Heat oil in a wok and fry the spice paste until fragrant.

- Put in the squid, sour star fruit, lime juice and cook for 3 minutes.

- Add tomato sauce, sugar and mint leaves and stir well. Season with salt to taste.

- Garnish with mint leaves and serve immediately.

MUM'S DRIED SQUID IN CHILLI SAUCE
SAMBAL SOTONG KERING EMAK

When I was a child, my mother cooked this *sambal* once a month, on my father's pay day. Dried squid was expensive in those days, and this dish was a special treat for our family. Typically dried squid has to be soaked in *air kapur* (alkaline water) overnight before cooking, but today it can be bought ready-to-cook. I love the flavour of the peanuts as well as the sweetness of this *sambal*. It tastes wonderful with *nasi lemak*.

Cooking oil 6 Tbsp

Dried squid 4, large, soaked in alkaline water overnight, drained and cut into bite-size pieces

Salt to taste

Sugar to taste

Water 4 Tbsp

Tamarind juice 375 ml (12 fl oz / 1¹/₂ cup), made from 2¹/₂ Tbsp tamarind pulp mixed with 375 ml (12 fl oz / 1¹/₂ cup) water and strained

Peanuts 170 g (6 oz), roasted and coarsely pounded

Spice paste

Dried chillies 40, seeded, soaked in water and drained

Dried prawn (shrimp) paste (*belacan*) 1 tsp

Shallots 15, peeled

- Combine ingredients for spice paste in a food processor and blend until smooth. Heat oil in a wok over medium heat and sauté the spice paste until the oil separates and the mixture is fragrant.

- Add the squid, salt, sugar and water. Simmer for 20 minutes until the squid is soft. Add the tamarind juice and peanuts. Cook until the gravy thickens.

STUFFED SQUID
KETUPAT SOTONG

Glutinous rice 400 g (14 oz), rinsed, soaked and drained

Coconut milk 250 ml (8 fl oz / 1 cup), extracted from 1 grated coconut and 250 ml (8 fl oz / 1 cup) water

Squid 500 g (1 lb 1½ oz), cleaned, cartilage and ink sac removed

Cocktail sticks a few

Coconut milk 250 ml (8 fl oz / 1 cup), extracted from 1 coconut and 250 ml (8 fl oz / 1 cup) water

Fenugreek 1 tsp

Mustard seeds 1 Tbsp

Lemongrass 1 stalk, bruised

Salt to taste

Sugar to taste

Red chillies 1, seeded and sliced

Spring onions (scallions) 1, finely sliced

Pounded ingredients

Lemongrass 1 stalk, sliced

Shallots 3, peeled

Ginger 1-cm (½-in) knob, peeled

- Combine glutinous rice and coconut milk and steam for 30 minutes or until cooked. Remove and set aside to cool.

- Stuff squids with rice and secure with cocktail sticks. Set aside.

- Pour the coconut milk into a pot. Add the pounded ingredients, fenugreek and mustard seeds and bring to the boil.

- Put in the stuffed squid and bruised lemongrass. Season with salt and sugar and simmer until gravy thickens.

- Garnish with chillies and spring onions. Serve immediately.

CUTTLEFISH IN PEANUT SAMBAL
SAMBAL SOTONG BERKACANG

Vegetable oil 4 Tbsp

Tamarind juice 4 Tbsp, made from 1 Tbsp tamarind pulp mixed with 4 Tbsp water

Coconut milk (optional) 125 ml (4 fl oz / ½ cup), extracted from ½ coconut and 125 ml (4 fl oz / ½ cup) water and strained

Salt to taste

Sugar to taste

Coarsely ground peanuts 3 Tbsp

Cuttlefish 1, cleaned and soaked until softened, then sliced

Spice paste

Shallots 8, peeled

Garlic 2 cloves, peeled

Dried prawn (shrimp) paste (*belacan*) ½ Tbsp

Ground chilli paste 4 Tbsp

Onion 1, peeled and sliced

- Combine ingredients for spice paste in a food processor and blend until smooth. Heat oil in a wok and sauté the spice paste until fragrant.

- Pour in the tamarind juice, coconut milk (if using), salt and sugar.

- Cook over low heat until the gravy thickens, then add the peanuts.

- Put in the cuttlefish and cook for 2 minutes before turning off the heat.

- Serve with rice or *nasi lemak*.

FRAGRANT FRIED SQUID
SOTONG GORENG SRI WANGI

Squid 500 g (1 lb 1½ oz), cleaned and sliced

Cooking oil for deep-frying + 1 Tbsp

Lemongrass 2 stalks, finely sliced

Torch ginger bud 1, finely sliced

Bird's eye chillies (*cili padi*) 10, seeded and sliced

***Tom yam* paste** 2 Tbsp

Water 4 Tbsp

Honey 1 tsp

Mayonnaise 1½ Tbsp

Kaffir lime leaves 3, finely sliced

Marinade

Oyster sauce 1½ Tbsp

Salt to taste

Egg 1, medium, beaten

Corn flour (cornstarch) 3 Tbsp

- Combine ingredients for the marinade in a bowl and stir well to combine. Add the squid to the marinade and set aside for 15 minutes.

- Heat oil in a wok and deep-fry the squid until golden brown and crisp. Drain.

- In a clean wok, heat 1 Tbsp oil and sauté the lemongrass, torch ginger bud, chillies and *tom yam* paste until fragrant.

- Add water, honey and squid and stir well. Remove from heat and stir in mayonnaise. Garnish with kaffir lime leaves and serve warm with rice.

COCKLE RENDANG
RENDANG KERANG

Cooking oil 4 Tbsp

Coconut milk 1 litre (32 fl oz / 4 cups), extracted from 1½ grated coconuts and 1 litre (32 fl oz / 4 cups) water

Dried sour fruit (*asam gelugor*) 3 pieces

Turmeric leaf 1, finely sliced

Kaffir lime leaf 1, finely sliced

Cockle meat 600 g (1 lb 5 oz)

Salt to taste

Sugar to taste

Pounded roasted grated or desiccated coconut (*kerisik*) 55 g (2 oz)

Spice paste

Dried chillies 10, seeded, soaked in water and drained

Bird's eye chillies (*cili padi*) 5, seeded

Lemongrass 2 stalks, finely sliced

Shallots 5, peeled

Garlic 1 clove, peeled

Ginger 1-cm (½-in) knob, peeled

Galangal 1-cm (½-in) knob, peeled

Turmeric 1-cm (½-in) knob, peeled

- Combine ingredients for the spice paste in a food processor and blend until smooth. Heat oil in a wok and sauté the spice paste until almost dry.

- Pour in coconut milk and add the dried sour fruit, turmeric leaf and kaffir lime leaf. Simmer until gravy thickens.

- Add the cockle meat and season with salt and sugar. Simmer until cockle meat is cooked.

- Add grated coconut and simmer for 5 minutes over medium heat. Serve warm with rice.

169

NOTE

To make fish stock, boil fish head, tail and fins in 2 litres (64 fl oz / 8 cups) water and allow to simmer for 15 minutes. Strain and discard fish parts. You can also dissolve fish stock granules in water according to manufacturer's directions for the quantity needed.

CHILLI FRIED CLAMS
LALA TUMIS PEDAS

Peanut oil 4 Tbsp

Lemongrass 2 stalks, bruised

Preserved soy beans (*tau cheo*) 2 Tbsp

Oyster sauce 2 Tbsp

Clams 500 g (1 lb 1½ oz), washed and drained

Fish stock or water 250 ml (8 fl oz / 1 cup)

Corn flour (cornstarch) 1 tsp, mixed with 1 Tbsp water

Spring onions (scallions) 6, cut into 2-cm (1-in) lengths

Sugar ½ tsp

Red chillies 2, seeded and sliced

Spice paste

Red chillies 5, seeded

Garlic 4 cloves, peeled

Ginger 2-cm (1-in) knob, peeled

- Combine ingredients for spice paste in a food processor and blend until smooth. Heat oil in a wok and sauté the spice paste and lemongrass until fragrant.

- Add the preserved soy beans, oyster sauce and clams. Stir well and cover tightly.

- After 2–3 minutes, remove the lid and make sure that all the clams have opened. Discard any that do not open. Stir in the fish stock or water, corn flour mixture and spring onions. Season with sugar and bring the gravy to a simmer.

- When the gravy thickens, remove from heat. Garnish with sliced chillies and serve immediately.

COCONUT SNAILS WITH YAM STEMS

GULAI SIPUT HISAP BERSAMA KELADI

Yam stems 500 g (1 lb 1^1/$_2$ oz), peeled and cut into 5-cm (2-in) lengths

Coconut milk 125 ml (4 fl oz / 1 cup), extracted from ^{1}/$_2$ grated coconut and 125 ml (4 fl oz / 1 cup) water

Coconut snails (*siput hisap*) 1 kg (2 lb 3 oz)

Dried sour fruit (*asam gelugor*) 2 pieces

Turmeric 1-cm (^{1}/$_2$-in) knob, peeled and finely ground

Bird's eye chillies (*cili padi*) 10, seeded and sliced

Thick coconut milk 250 ml (8 fl oz / 1 cup), extracted from 3 coconuts and 250 ml (8 fl oz / 1 cup) water

Salt to taste

- Boil yam stems for about 10 minutes until soft. Discard water.

- In the same pot, pour in coconut milk, coconut snails, dried sour fruit, turmeric and chillies.

- Boil for about 5 minutes, then add in thick coconut milk. Allow to simmer for a few minutes. Season with salt and serve warm.

SEAFOOD OTAK-OTAK IN COCONUT
OTAK-OTAK MAKANAN LAUT

Young coconut 1

Cooking oil 2 Tbsp

Thai red curry paste 2 Tbsp

Spanish mackerel 400 g (14 oz), deboned and finely chopped

Prawns (shrimps) 300 g (10½ oz), shelled, deveined and finely chopped

Coconut milk 250 ml (8 fl oz / 1 cup), extracted from ½ grated coconut and 250 ml (8 fl oz / 1 cup) water

Crabmeat 300 g (10½ oz)

Galangal 1-cm (½-in) knob, peeled and finely sliced

Kaffir lime leaves 3, finely sliced

Basil leaves 1 sprig, finely sliced

Fish sauce 1 Tbsp

Lime juice 2 tsp

Sugar 1 tsp

Red chilli 1, seeded and finely sliced

Chopped coriander leaves (cilantro) 2 Tbsp

Corn flour (cornstarch) 1 tsp

Pounded roasted grated or desiccated coconut (kerisik) 1 Tbsp

- Cut through the top of the coconut and scoop out the flesh. Set aside.

- Heat oil in a wok and fry the Thai red curry paste until fragrant. Add the fish and prawns and stir well.

- Add the remaining ingredients, including the reserved coconut flesh. Mix well and transfer into the coconut shell.

- Bake in a preheated at 180°C (350°F) oven for 30 minutes until the *otak-otak* boils and becomes almost dry. Garnish as desired and serve immediately.

SALADS & VEGETABLES

FIDDLEHEAD FERN SALAD WITH COCKLES
KERABU PUCUK PAKU BERSAMA KERANG

Bottled *sambal belacan* 3 Tbsp

Grated palm sugar (*gula melaka*) 2 Tbsp

Kalamansi limes 3, juice extracted

Salt to taste

Fiddlehead ferns 300 g (10½ oz), blanched lightly in boiling water, drained and plunged in cold water

Cockles 500 g (1 lb 1½ oz), soaked in boiling water for 1 minute, flesh removed and set aside

Shallots 10, peeled and thinly sliced

Pounded roasted grated or desiccated coconut (*kerisik*) 6 Tbsp

- Combine *sambal belacan*, palm sugar, lime juice and salt to taste in a bowl and stir well to combine.

- Add the remaining ingredients and toss well. Serve immediately.

PENANG ROJAK
ROJAK PULAU PINANG

Young mangoes 2, peeled and cut into bite-size pieces

Rose apples (*jambu air*) 4, cut into bite-size pieces

Cucumbers 4, cut into bite-size pieces

Yam bean 1, peleed and cut into bite-size pieces

Semi-ripe papaya ½, peeled and cut into bite-size pieces

Sauce

Brown sugar 3 Tbsp

Tamarind juice 125 ml (4 fl oz / ½ cup), squeezed from 2 Tbsp of tamarind and 125 ml (4 fl oz / ½ cup) water and strained

Dried prawn (shrimp) paste (*belacan*) 1-cm (½-in), toasted

Peanuts 5 Tbsp, toasted + more for topping

White sesame seeds 1 Tbsp, toasted + more to sprinkle over

Salt ¾ tsp

Black prawn (shrimp) paste (*hae ko*) 3–4 Tbsp

- Combine ingredients for sauce in a bowl and stir well to combine.

- Place all the fruit in a salad bowl. Pour sauce over and toss the fruit with the sauce thoroughly.

- Sprinkle over with more peanuts and sesame seeds on top just before serving. Serve immediately after sauce has been mixed or sauce will become watery.

PINEAPPLE AND CUCUMBER SALAD
ACAR MENTAH

Ripe pineapple ½, peeled and thinly sliced

Cucumber 1, peeled, cored and thinly sliced

Kaffir lime leaves 2, finely sliced

Torch ginger bud ½, finely sliced

Onion 1, peeled and thinly sliced

Spice paste

Dried prawn (shrimp) paste (*belacan*) 2-cm (1-in), toasted

Red chillies 2, seeded

Dried prawns (shrimps) 100 g (3½ oz), soaked and drained

Salt to taste

Sugar to taste

Kalamansi lime juice to taste

- Combine ingredients for spice paste in a mortar and pound until smooth.

- Mix the pineapple and cucumber slices with the pounded ingredients in a bowl. Toss well.

- Garnish with kaffir lime leaves, torch ginger bud and onion. Serve immediately.

JACKFRUIT AND FERMENTED SOY BEAN CAKE SALAD
KERABU NANGKA DAN TEMPE

Peanut oil 4 Tbsp

Coconut milk 250 ml (8 fl oz / 1 cup), extracted from 1 grated coconut and 250 ml (8 fl oz / 1 cup) water

Grated palm sugar (*gula melaka*) 2 Tbsp

Salt to taste

Lime 1, squeezed for juice

Turmeric leaf 1, finely sliced

Young jackfruit 200 g (7 oz), diced and blanched in salted water until soft

Fermented soy bean cakes (*tempe*) 3, fried and diced

Firm bean curd 1, fried and diced

Long beans 8, blanched in hot water for 1 minute, then finely sliced

Crisp-fried shallots 60 g (2 oz)

Grated coconut 60 g (2 oz), dry-fried until golden

Pineapple 1/4, peeled and diced

Spice paste

Red chillies 5, seeded

Bird's eye chillies (*cili padi*) 6, seeded

Shallots 8, peeled

Lesser galangal 1-cm (1/2-in) knob, peeled

Candlenuts 4

Lemongrass 2 stalks

Turmeric 2-cm (1-in) knob, peeled

Black peppercorns 1 tsp

Dried prawns (shrimps) 2 Tbsp, soaked and drained

Galangal 1-cm (1/2-in) knob, peeled

Kaffir lime leaf 1, central vein removed and shredded

- Combine ingredients for spice paste in a food processor and blend until smooth. Heat oil in a wok and fry the spice paste until fragrant.

- Add coconut milk, palm sugar, salt and cook until the gravy thickens. Remove from heat and leave to cool slightly.

- Pour young jackfruit, fermented soy bean cake, and long beans into a bowl and mix with the remaining ingredients. For a spicier version, add more sliced bird's eye chillies. Serve immediately.

VEGETABLE SALAD
SAYUR PECAL

Vegetable oil 4 Tbsp

Tamarind pulp 2 Tbsp, seeds removed

Water 375 ml (12 fl oz / 1½ cups)

Shallots 10, peeled and sliced

Dried chillies 15, soaked in water, seeded and drained

Dried prawn (shrimp) paste (*belacan*) 1 Tbsp

Peanuts 300 g (10½ oz), roasted and coarsely ground

Brown sugar 6 Tbsp

Sugar 5 Tbsp

Salt to taste

Bean sprouts 100 g (3½ oz), tailed

Water convolvulus 100 g (3½ oz), cut into 5-cm (2-in) lengths

Long beans 150 g (5⅓ oz), cut into 5-cm (2-in) lengths

Cucumber 1, peeled, cored and thinly sliced

Yam bean 1, peeled and cut into thin strips

Firm bean curd 2 pieces, fried and cubed

Hard-boiled eggs 2, peeled and quartered

Fermented soy bean cakes (*tempe*) 3, fried and cut into cubes

Potatoes (optional) 2, boiled, peeled and sliced

Prawn crackers (optional) 55 g (2 oz)

- Heat 1 Tbsp oil in a wok and fry tamarind pulp for 1 minute.
- Mix the pulp with 125 ml (4 fl oz / ½ cup) water and stir well. Strain the juice.
- Heat the remaining oil and fry the shallots, dried chillies and dried prawn paste. Remove and put the fried ingredients into a food processor and grind to a paste.
- Meanwhile, combine peanuts, brown sugar, sugar, tamarind juice and the remaining water in a pot. Simmer the sauce until slightly thick, then add salt.
- Blanch all the vegetables, except the cucumber abd yam bean, in boiling salted water for a few minutes.
- Drain and arrange in a dish together with the cucumber, bean curd, eggs, fermented soy bean cake, potatoes and prawn crackers.
- Serve vegetables with the sauce.

CHUBB MACKEREL SALAD
KERABU IKAN KEMBUNG

Chubb mackerel 6, cleaned and deep-fried until crisp

Shallots 6, peeled and finely sliced

Red chillies 2, seeded and finely chopped

Bird's eye chillies (*cili padi*) 4, seeded and sliced

Peanuts 85 g (3 oz), roasted and pounded

Unripe mangoes 2, peeled and finely grated

Limes 2–3, juice extracted

Torch ginger bud 1, sliced

Mint leaves a handful, finely chopped

Fish sauce 3 Tbsp

Tomatoes 2, finely diced

Sugar 1 tsp

Lemongrass 1 stalk, finely sliced

- Bone and shred the fish and toss with the remaining ingredients until well mixed. Serve immediately.

BEAN SPROUTS AND TRIPE SALAD
KERABU TAUGE DAN PERUT

Tripe 200 g (7 oz), boiled in water for 2 hours, drained and sliced

Bean sprouts 200 g, (7 oz) tailed and blanched

Shallots 8, peeled and thinly sliced

Sambal belacan 3 Tbsp, made from 3 red chillies + ¹/₂ tsp toasted dried prawn (shrimp) paste (*belacan*)

Pounded roasted grated or desiccated coconut (*kerisik*) 4 Tbsp

Kalamansi limes 4, juice extracted

Uncooked rice 3 Tbsp, toasted and coarsely pounded

Store-bought coconut cream 2 Tbsp

Salt to taste

Sugar to taste

• Put all the ingredients into a bowl and mix well. Serve immediately.

PRAWN AND MANGO SALAD
KERABU UDANG DAN MANGGA MUDA

This salad inspired by the famous *som tam* (papaya salad) of Thailand. Besides freshwater prawns, the Thais also like to use freshwater catfish (*Clarias batrachus*). This salad goes well on top of deep-fried catfish. If catfish is not available, grouper or sea bass can be used.

Freshwater prawns (shrimps) 500 g (1 lb 1½ oz), cleaned, shelled, blanched and drained

Green mangoes 2, peeled and finely grated

Kaffir lime leaves 2, finely sliced

Chopped coriander leaves (cilantro) 15 g (½ oz)

Chopped mint leaves 2 Tbsp

Fish sauce 4 Tbsp

Limes 2, juice extracted

Salt to taste

Sugar to taste

Glass noodles 200 g (7 oz), blanched and drained

Crisp-fried shallots 55 g (2 oz)

Salad greens as needed

Peanuts 85 g (3 oz), roasted and pounded

Spice paste

Red chillies 3, seeded

Bird's eye chillies (*cili padi*) 3, seeded

Dried prawns (shrimps) 45 g (1½ oz), soaked in water and drained

Garlic 3 cloves, peeled

Grated palm sugar (*gula melaka*) or brown sugar 3 Tbsp

Tomatoes 2, quartered

- Combine ingredients for spice paste in a food processor and blend until fine.

- Mix all the ingredients except salad greens and peanuts, together with the prepared spice paste.

- Line a serving dish with salad greens, place the salad on top and sprinkle with peanuts. Serve immediately.

INDIAN SALAD
PASEMBOR

Bean sprouts 100 g (3½ oz), blanched

Cucumber 1, peeled and julienned

Yam bean 1, peeled and cut into thin strips

Hard-boiled eggs 2, peeled and halved

Fried bean curd 4 pieces, thinly sliced

Lettuce leaves as needed

Sauce

Vegetable oil 4 Tbsp

Shallots 4, peeled and minced

Garlic 3 cloves, peeled

Ground chilli paste 2 Tbsp

Curry powder 2 Tbsp

Sweet potatoes 300 g (10½ oz), boiled, peeled and mashed

Palm sugar (*gula melaka*) 40 g (1⅓ oz), grated

Water 500 ml (16 fl oz / 2 cups)

Salt to taste

Sugar to taste

White sesame seeds 4 Tbsp, toasted and coarsely crushed

Coconut fritters

Cooking oil for deep-frying

Rice flour 75 g (2⅔ oz)

Plain (all-purpose) flour 60 g (2 oz)

Grated coconut 70 g (2½ oz)

Onion 1, peeled and chopped

Egg 1, beaten

Salt a pinch

Water as needed

Prawn fritters

Plain (all-purpose) flour 180 g (6½ oz), sifted

Baking powder 1 tsp, sifted

Egg 1, beaten

Water enough to form a thick batter

Bean sprouts 55 g (2 oz), tailed

Prawns (shrimps) 150 g (5⅓ oz), peeled and deveined

Turmeric powder 1½ tsp

Salt 1 tsp

- Prepare sauce. Heat oil in a wok and fry the shallots, garlic, chilli paste and curry powder until fragrant. Add the mashed sweet potatoes, palm sugar and water. Simmer and season with salt and sugar. Cook the sauce until slightly thick. Stir in sesame seeds. Set aside.

- Prepare coconut fritters. In a clean wok, heat oil for deep-frying. Combine all the other ingredients for the coconut fritters to form a thick batter. Spoon a ladleful of batter and drop into the hot oil. Fry the fritters until golden brown. Leave to cool and slice into bite-size pieces.

- Prepare prawn fritters. Mix the flour and baking powder. Add the egg and sufficient water to make a thick batter. Fold in all the other ingredients. Fry as with coconut fritters. Leave to cool and slice into bite-size pieces.

- Arrange bean sprouts, cucumber, yam bean, eggs, fried bean curd, sliced coconut fritters and chopped prawn fritters on a bed of lettuce. Pour the sauce over and serve immediately.

FOUR-ANGLED BEAN SALAD
KERABU KACANG BOTOL

Cooking oil 4 Tbsp

Prawns (shrimps) 300 g (10½ oz), cleaned and shelled with tails intact

Four-angled beans 400 g (14 oz), sliced

Kalamansi lime 1, juice extracted

Salt to taste

Sugar to taste

Spice paste

Red chillies 6, seeded

Shallots 5, peeled

Dried prawn (shrimp) paste (*belacan*) 1 tsp

Dried prawns (shrimps) 2 Tbsp, soaked and drained

- Combine ingredients for spice paste in a food processor and blend until smooth.
- Heat oil in a wok and fry the spice paste until fragrant. Put in the prawns and stir-fry for a couple of minutes before adding four-angled beans. Stir to combine.
- Season with lime juice, salt and sugar. Serve hot.

MIXED VEGETABLE PICKLE
ACAR RAMPAI

Cucumber 1, peeled, halved, cored and julienned

Carrot 1, peeled and julienned

Water as needed

Salt 1 Tbsp + more to taste

Cooking oil 4 Tbsp

Green chillies 2, seeded and sliced

Red chillies 2, seeded and sliced

Shallots 5, peeled and sliced

Garlic 5 cloves, peeled and chopped

White sesame seeds 4 Tbsp, toasted

White vinegar 4 Tbsp

Sugar 3 Tbsp

Spice paste

Candlenuts 6

Ground chilli paste 3 Tbsp

Turmeric 1-cm (½-in) knob, peeled

Garlic 2 cloves, peeled

- Soak the cucumber and carrot in water mixed with 1 Tbsp salt for 1 hour. Drain and dry the vegetables with a tea towel.

- Combine ingredients for spice paste in a food processor and blend until smooth. Heat oil in a wok and fry the spice paste until fragrant.

- Add the cucumber, carrot, chillies, shallots and garlic and stir-fry for a few minutes.

- Add vinegar, salt and sugar to taste. Toss in sesame seeds and remove from heat.

BANANA FLOWER AND COCKLE SALAD
KERABU JANTUNG BERSAMA KERANG

Banana flower 300 g (10½ oz),
boiled and sliced

Dried prawn (shrimp) paste
(*belacan*) 1 tsp

Red chillies 4, seeded, finely sliced

Coconut milk 125 ml (8 fl oz /
½ cup), extracted from 2
coconuts and 125 ml (4 fl oz /
½ cup) water

Limes 3, juice extracted

**Pounded roasted grated or
desiccated coconut** (*kerisik*) 4 tsp

Shallots 10, peeled and finely sliced

Cockle meat 600 g (1 lb 5 oz)

Dried shrimps 100 g (3½ oz), soaked,
drained and finely pounded

- Put all the ingredients in a bowl. Stir well to combine.
  Serve immediately.

CUTTLEFISH SALAD
KERABU SOTONG

Cuttlefish 500 g (1 lb 1½ oz), cut into bite-size pieces, boiled and chilled

Unripe mango 1, peeled and shredded

Dried prawns (shrimps) 30 g (1 oz), fried

Shallot 1, peeled and finely sliced

Lemongrass 2 stalks, finely sliced

Kaffir lime leaves 2, central stems removed and finely sliced

Mint leaves a handful, chopped

Red chillies 1, seeded and finely sliced

Dressing

Fish sauce 2 Tbsp

Sugar 2 Tbsp

Garlic 3 cloves, peeled and finely chopped

White sesame seeds 2 Tbsp, toasted

Kalamansi limes 2, juice extracted

Light soy sauce 2 Tbsp

- Combine ingredients for dressing in a bowl and stir to mix well.
- Put all the salad ingredients in a bowl. Add in the dressing and toss well to combine. Garnish with sliced chillies and a sprig of mint. Serve immediately.

PINEAPPLE CHUTNEY
CUTNI NANAS

Pineapple 1, peeled and sliced

Turmeric powder 1 Tbsp

Ghee 70 g (2¹/₂ oz)

Cinnamon stick 10-cm (4-in)

Cardamom pods 4

Cloves 4

Star anise 2

Ginger 2-cm (1-in) knob, peeled and thinly sliced

Onion ¹/₂, peeled and thinly sliced

Garlic 2 cloves, peeled and finely chopped

Red chillies 4, seeded and pounded to a paste + 2, seeded and quartered lengthwise for garnishing

Dried prawns (shrimps) 4 Tbsp, soaked, drained and finely pounded

Mustard seeds 2 tsp

Water 250 ml (8 fl oz / 1 cup)

Castor sugar 6 Tbsp

White vinegar 2 Tbsp

Tamarind juice 3 Tbsp, made from 1 Tbsp tamarind pulp mixed with 3 Tbsp water and strained

Mango chutney 4 Tbsp

Salt to taste

- Mix the pineapple with turmeric powder until well coated. Set aside.
- Heat ghee in a wok and sauté cinnamon, cardamom pods, cloves, star anise and ginger, onion and garlic until golden brown.
- Add the pounded red chillies, dried prawns and mustard seeds. Cook over medium heat until fragrant.
- Add the pineapple, water, sugar, vinegar, *tamarind juice* and mango chutney. Stir well to combine. Bring to the boil and simmer until the gravy is thick. Garnish with red chillies and serve immediately.

STIR-FRIED FOUR-ANGLED BEANS WITH SAMBAL
SAMBAL GORENG KACANG BOTOL

Cooking oil 4 Tbsp

Freshwater prawns (shrimps) 300 g (10½ oz), cleaned and shelled with tails intact

Four-angled beans 400 g (14 oz), sliced

Kalamansi lime 1, juice extracted

Salt to taste

Sugar to taste

Spice paste

Red chillies 6, seeded

Shallots 5, peeled

Dried prawn (shrimp) paste (*belacan*) 1 tsp

Dried prawns (shrimps) 2 Tbsp, soaked and drained

- Combine ingredients for spice paste in a food processor and blend until smooth.

- Heat oil in a wok and fry the spice paste until fragrant. Put in the prawns and stir for a couple of minutes before adding the four-angled beans. Stir to combine.

- Season with lime juice, salt and sugar. Serve hot.

YAM IN FERMENTED DURIAN
GULAI KELADI ASAM TEMPOYAK

Yam 300 g (10¹/₂ oz), peeled and cut into large wedges

Yam stems 4, peeled, boiled for 2 minutes with 2 pieces of dried sour fruit, then drained

Water 800 ml (27 fl oz)

Laksa leaves 9

Torch ginger bud 1, halved lengthwise

Fermented durian 8 Tbsp

Salt to taste

Sugar to taste

Spice paste

Red chillies 4, seeded

Bird's eye chillies (*cili padi*) 15, seeded

Turmeric 2-cm (1-in) knob, peeled and chopped

- Pound ingredients for spice paste using a mortar and pestle until smooth.
- Put all the ingredients except salt and sugar in a pot and slowly bring to the boil.
- When yam is tender, season with salt and sugar. Serve warm.

STIR-FRIED AUBERGINES WITH PRAWN PASTE
TERUNG GORENG SAMBAL UDANG

Cooking oil for shallow-frying

Aubergines (eggplants/brinjals) 2, cut into 5-cm (2-in) lengths

Prawns (shrimps) 100 g (3½ oz), cleaned and shelled

Salt to taste

Sugar to taste

Water 3 Tbsp

Spice paste

Dried chillies 15, seeded and soaked to soften

Shallots 8, peeled

Garlic 2 cloves, peeled

Dried prawn (shrimp) paste (*belacan*) 1 tsp

Dried prawns (shrimps) 4 Tbsp

Sweet soy sauce 1 Tbsp

Oyster sauce 1 Tbsp

Thick tamarind paste 1 Tbsp

- Heat oil in a wok and shallow-fry aubergines for a few minutes. Remove and set aside.

- Combine ingredients for spice paste in a food processor and blend until smooth. Heat some oil in a clean wok and fry the spice paste until fragrant.

- Add the aubergines and prawns. Season with salt and sugar. Add water to soften the aubergines and lower heat and cook until soft. Serve warm with rice.

BEAN CURD AND BEAN SPROUTS IN COCONUT GRAVY

MASAK LEMAK TAUHU DAN TAUGE

Shallots 10, peeled and finely sliced

Anchovies (*ikan bilis*) 15 g (¹/₂ oz)

Coconut milk 250 ml (8 fl oz / 1 cup),
extracted from 1 grated coconut
and 250 ml (8 fl oz / 1 cup) water

Bean sprouts 500 g (1 lb 1¹/₂ oz),
tailed

Bean curd 3 pieces, deep-fried and
cut into 8 pieces

Chinese chives 100 g (3¹/₂ oz), cut
into 2.5-cm (1-in) lengths

Store-bought coconut cream 500 ml
(16 fl oz / 2 cups)

Salt to taste

- Put shallots, anchovies and coconut milk in a pot and
  bring to the boil.

- Add bean sprouts, bean curd, Chinese chives and
  coconut cream. Season with salt.

- Remove from heat once cooked. Serve immediately.

SWEET LEAF WITH SWEET POTATO
GULAI PUCUK MANIS BERSAMA KELEDEK

Coconut milk 500 ml (16 fl oz / 2 cups), extracted from 1¹⁄₂ grated coconuts 500 ml (16 fl oz / 2 cups) water, and then squeezed again for 250 ml (8 fl oz / 1 cup) second-squeeze coconut milk using 250 ml (8 fl oz / 1 cup) water

Sweet potato 1, about 300 g (10¹⁄₂ oz), peeled and cut into cubes

Shallots 10, peeled and thinly sliced

Anchovies (*ikan bilis*) 125 g (4¹⁄₂ oz)

Sweet leaf (*pucuk manis*) 200 g (7 oz)

Salt to taste

- Heat second-squeeze coconut milk in a pot and bring to the boil. Add sweet potato, shallots and anchovies.

- When the potatoes are soft, add sweet leaves.

- Add the first-squeeze coconut milk and boil for about 5 minutes, then switch off heat. Add salt to taste and serve immediately.

RICE & NOODLES

HERB RICE SALAD
NASI ULAM

Cooked rice 2 kg (4 lb 6 oz)

Bottled *sambal belacan* 3 Tbsp

Salted egg 1, boiled, shelled and crushed

Shallots 6, peeled and thinly sliced

Young ginger 1-cm (1/2-in) knob, peeled and thinly sliced

Torch ginger bud 1/2, finely sliced

Selom **leaves** *(pucuk selom)* 30 g (1 oz), finely sliced

Wild pepper leaves *(daun kadok)* 30 g (1 oz), finely sliced

Cosmos plant shoots *(ulam raja)* 30 g (1 oz), finely sliced

Laksa **leaves** 30, finely sliced

Turmeric leaves 3, finely sliced

Lemongrass 2, finely sliced

Salted threadfin *(ikan kurau)* 55 g (2 oz), fried and pounded

Mackerel 2, grilled and flaked

Grated coconut 125 g (4 1/2 oz), dry-fried until golden brown + 1 Tbsp, dry-fried and pounded to make *kerisik*

Kalamansi limes 3, juice extracted

* Mix all the ingredients in a large bowl. Toss well and serve immediately.

KAMPUNG-STYLE FRIED RICE
NASI GORENG KAMPUNG

Vegetable oil 125 ml (4 fl oz / ½ cup)

Light soy sauce 2 Tbsp

Thick sweet soy sauce 3 Tbsp

Oyster sauce 2 Tbsp

Salt to taste

Sugar to taste

Stink beans 10, peeled

Chicken breast 100 g (3½ oz), thinly sliced

Prawns (shrimps) 150 g (5⅓ oz), cleaned and shelled

Cooked rice 300 g (10½ oz)

Water convolvulus 55 g (2 oz) washed and plucked

Dried whitebait 30 g (1 oz), cleaned, washed, drained and fried

Bottled *sambal belacan* as needed

Kalamansi limes 1–2, halved

Spice paste

Red chillies 4, seeded

Bird's eye chillies *(cili padi)* 5, seeded

Shallots 6, peeled

Dried prawn (shrimp) paste *(belacan)* 1 tsp

Dried prawns (shrimps) 3 Tbsp, soaked and drained

- Combine ingredients for spice paste in a food processor and blend until smooth.

- Heat oil in a wok and sauté the spice paste until fragrant. Add light soy sauce, thick sweet soy sauce, oyster sauce, salt, sugar, stink beans, chicken, prawns and rice. Stir well to combine, then continue frying for 5 minutes until heated through.

- Put in the water convolvulus and fried whitebait. Serve with *sambal belacan* and limes.

MUM'S FRIED RICE
NASI GORENG EMAK

Cooking oil 3–4 Tbsp

Finely minced garlic 2 tsp

Finely minced shallots 1 Tbsp

Ground chilli paste 2 Tbsp

Anchovies *(ikan bilis)* 150 g (5$\frac{1}{3}$ oz), pounded

Eggs 2

Cooked rice 500 g (1 lb 1$\frac{1}{2}$ oz)

Salt to taste

Sugar to taste

- Heat oil in a wok and stir-fry the garlic, shallots and chilli paste until dry and fragrant.

- Add the anchovies and stir-fry for about 1 minute. Break the eggs into the wok and stir until cooked.

- Add rice and stir until thoroughly mixed.

- Season with salt and sugar. Remove from wok and garnish as desired. Serve immediately.

TOMATO RICE
NASI TOMATO

Ghee 125 ml (4 fl oz / ½ cup)

Garlic 2 cloves, peeled

Onion 1, large, peeled and finely sliced

Shallots 15, peeled and sliced

Lemongrass 2 stalks, bruised

Tomato paste 2 Tbsp

Raisins 4 Tbsp

Almonds 15

Cardamon pods 3

Cinnamon stick 2-cm (1-in)

Pandan leaves 2, shredded and knotted

Chicken stock (see Note on page 70) 500 ml (16 fl oz / 2 cups)

Evaporated milk 4 Tbsp

Rose water 3 Tbsp

Mint leaves 2, roughly chopped + more for garnishing

Salt to taste

Rice 500 g (1 lb 1½ oz), washed and rinsed

Crisp-fried shallots for garnishing

- Heat ghee in a saucepan and stir-fry the garlic, onion, shallots, lemongrass and tomato paste. Then add the raisins, almonds, cardamom pods, cinnamon and pandan leaves.

- Pour in chicken stock and evaporated milk. Then add rose water and mint leaves and bring to the boil. Season with salt to taste.

- Add rice and boil until cooked. Garnish with crisp-fried shallots and mint leaves. Serve immediately.

RICE PILAF
NASI MINYAK

Ghee 125 ml (4 fl oz / ½ cup)

Shallots 10, peeled and sliced

Garlic 3 cloves, peeled and sliced

Pandan leaves 2, shredded and knotted

Cinnamon stick 2-cm (1-in)

Star anise 2

Cardamom pods 4

Cloves 6

Almonds 10

Chicken stock (see Note on page 70) 125 ml (4 fl oz / ½ cup)

Evaporated milk 4 Tbsp

Basmati rice 125 g (4½ oz), washed

Rose water 4 Tbsp

- Heat ghee in a saucepan and stir-fry the shallots, garlic, pandan leaves, cinnamon, star anise, cardamom, cloves and almonds until fragrant.
- Pour in the chicken stock and evaporated milk. Add the rice and rose water and boil until rice is cooked.

RICE COOKED IN COCONUT MILK
NASI LEMAK

Rice 600 g (1 lb 5 oz), washed and drained

Coconut milk 1.1 litres (37 fl oz), extracted from 2 grated coconuts and 1.1 litres (37 fl oz) water

Ginger 1-cm (2-in) knob, peeled and thinly sliced

Pandan leaves 3, knotted

Salt 1 tsp

Peanuts 70 g (2½ oz), fried until golden

Anchovies *(ikan bilis)* 55 g (2 oz), washed, drained and deep-fried until crispy

Hard-boiled eggs 3, peeled and quartered

- Combine rice with the coconut milk, ginger and pandan leaves in a pot. Season with salt and bring to the boil until all the liquid has been absorbed. Stir well.

- Reduce heat and cover pot. Leave to cook for another 10 minutes.

- Serve with fried peanuts, anchovies, hard-boiled eggs and Prawns with Sambal Belacan (see page 144).

BIRYANI RICE
NASI BERIANI GAM

Ghee 125 ml (4 fl oz / ½ cup)

Cardamom pods 4

Cloves 6

Star anise 2

Onion 1, large, peeled and chopped

Shallots 10, peeled and chopped

Garlic 4 cloves, peeled and finely minced

Ginger 2.5-cm (1-in) knob, peeled and finely minced

Lemongrass 2 stalks

Pandan leaves 2, knotted

Raisins 250 g (9 oz)

Tomatoes 2, roughly chopped

Chicken stock (see Note on page 70) 750 ml (24 fl oz / 3 cups)

Evaporated milk 250 ml (8 fl oz / 1 cup)

Saffron threads 1 tsp

Chopped mint 1 Tbsp + more for garnishing

Salt to taste

Basmati rice 1 kg (2 lb 3 oz), washed and rinsed

Rose water 4 Tbsp

Crisp-fried shallots for garnishing

- Heat ghee in a saucepan and stir-fry cardamom, cloves and star anise until fragrant. Add onion, shallots, garlic, ginger, lemongrass and pandan leaves and stir-fry for a few minutes. Stir in raisin and tomatoes and stir for about 10 minutes.

- Pour in chicken stock, evaporated milk, saffron and mint leaves. Bring to the boil. Add salt to taste and pour in rice. Leave to simmer until rice is cooked, about 20 minutes.

- Turn down the heat an cover saucepan. Cook for another 10 minutes. Stir in rose water and cook for 5 minutes.

- Garnish with mint leaves and serve with Chicken Kuzi (see page 90).

DAGANG RICE WITH TUNA CURRY
NASI DAGANG DAN GULAI IKAN TONGKOL

Rice 1 kg (2 lb 3 oz), soaked for a few hours, then washed and drained

Coconut milk 750 ml (24 fl oz / 3 cups), extracted from 1½ grated coconuts and 750 ml (24 fl oz / 3 cups) water

Fenugreek 2 tsp

Ginger 2.5-cm (1-in) knob, peeled and thinly sliced

Shallots 10, peeled and thinly sliced

Sugar 2 tsp

Salt 1 tsp

Tuna curry

Cooking oil 4 Tbsp

Coconut milk 750 ml (24 fl oz / 3 cups), extracted from 1½ grated coconuts and 750 ml (24 fl oz / 3 cups) water

Dried sour fruit (*asam gelugor*) 2 pieces

Tuna 350 g (12⅓ oz), cut into steaks

Salt to taste

Sugar to taste

Green chilli 1, seeded and halved

Red chilli 1, seeded and halved

Spice paste

Shallots 10, peeled

Turmeric 2.5-cm (1-in) knob, peeled

Galangal 2.5-cm (1-in) knob, peeled

Ground chilli paste 3 Tbsp

- Prepare tuna curry. Combine ingredients for spice paste in a food processor and blend until smooth. Heat oil in a wok and fry spice paste for a few minutes until fragrant. Add coconut milk and dried sour fruit and simmer for a few minutes. Add fish and season with salt and sugar. Add chillies and simmer for another 5 minutes or until fish is fully cooked.

- Prepare rice. Place rice in a steamer placed over boiling water and steam for 30 minutes. Transfer to a bowl and stir in coconut milk. Put the rice back into the steamer and cook for another 30 minutes.

- Transfer rice to the bowl again and add fenugreek, ginger, shallots, sugar and salt and continue steaming for another 20 minutes.

- Serve hot with prepared tuna curry.

CHEF WAN'S CHICKEN RICE
NASI AYAM CHEF WAN

Chicken 1, about 1.5 kg (3 lb 4½ oz), halved

Salt to taste

Freshly ground black pepper to taste

Ginger 2.5-cm (1-in) knob, peeled and pounded

Garlic 2 cloves, peeled and pounded

Thick sweet soy sauce 3 Tbsp

Margarine 3 Tbsp

Tomato for garnishing, sliced

Cucumber for garnishing, sliced

Coriander leaves (cilantro) a handful, chopped

Store-bought chilli sauce as needed

Chicken rice

Margarine 110 g (4 oz)

Onions 2, peeled and chopped

Young ginger 2-cm (1-in) knob, peeled and finely chopped

Garlic 3 cloves, peeled and finely chopped

Cinnamon stick 1-cm (½-in)

Cloves 4

Pandan leaves 2, shredded and knotted

Long grain rice 900 g (2 lb), washed and drained

Chicken stock (see Note on page 70) 1.4 litres (47 fl oz / 5½ cups)

Salt to taste

- Prepare chicken rice. Melt margarine in a wok and sauté the onions, ginger, garlic, cinnamon, cloves and pandan leaves for a few minutes until fragrant. Add the rice and stir-fry for a few minutes.

- Pour in the chicken stock and season with salt. Cook until the liquid is absorbed and then reduce heat. Cover and cook for another 10 minutes.

- Meanwhile, rub the chicken with salt, pepper, ginger, garlic, sweet soy sauce and margarine. Put on a baking tray.

- Bake in a preheated oven at 180°C (350°F) for 30–40 minutes until chicken is cooked.

- Cut the chicken into bite-size pieces and garnish with tomato, cucumber and coriander leaves. Serve with prepared rice and a side of chilli sauce.

MENADO VEGETABLE PORRIDGE
BUBUR MENEDO

Long grain rice 300 g (10¹/₂ oz),
washed and drained

Tapioca 300 g (10¹/₂ oz), peeled and
diced

Lemongrass 2 stalks, bruised

Ginger 3-cm (1¹/₂-in) knob, peeled
and finely chopped

Water as needed

Pumpkin 200 g (7 oz), peeled and
diced

Corn 3 ears, kernels extracted

Water convolvulus 300 g (10¹/₂ oz),
roughly chopped

Spinach 200 g (7 oz), roughly
chopped

Basil leaves a handful

Fried or roasted salted fish as
needed

Spring onion (scallion) as needed,
chopped

Chinese celery as needed, chopped

Crisp-fried shallots as needed

Tomato sambal

Red chillies 5, seeded

Dried prawn (shrimp) paste
(belacan) 2 tsp, roasted

Tomatoes 2, finely sliced

Kalamansi limes 2, juice extracted

- Prepare tomato *sambal*. Finely pound the chillies, prawn paste
  and tomatoes. Stir in the kalamansi lime juice. Set aside.

- To make porridge, boil the rice, tapioca, lemongrass and ginger
  in a pot of water until half-cooked. Add the pumpkin and
  corn kernels and boil until rice grains are broken up and the
  porridge is cooked. Add water as required during the cooking.

- About 5 minutes before serving, add the water convolvulus,
  spinach and basil leaves.

- Garnish with salted fish, spring onion, Chinese celery and crisp-
  fried shallots and serve with a side of prepared tomato *sambal*.

NOTE

Sliced red chillies and spring onions may also be used as garnish.

RICH RICE PORRIDGE
BUBUR ANEKA

Ghee 3 Tbsp

Garlic 3 cloves, peeled and finely chopped

Shallots 6, peeled and finely chopped

Pandan leaves 2, shredded and knotted

Star anise 2

Cloves 5

Cardamom pods 5

Cinnamon stick 2.5-cm (1-in)

Chicken breasts 2, diced

Long grain rice 450 g (1 lb), washed and drained

Dhal 100 g (3½ oz), soaked in water overnight and drained

Peanuts 85 g (3 oz)

Carrot 1, peeled and diced

Chicken stock cube 1, dissolved in 125 ml (4 fl oz / ½ cup) water

Coconut milk 500 ml (16 fl oz / 2 cups), extracted from 1 grated coconut and 500 ml (16 fl oz / 2 cups) water

Water as needed

Pounded roasted grated or desiccated coconut *(kerisik)* 55 g (2 oz)

Prawns (shrimps) 200 g (7 oz), cleaned and shelled

Salt to taste

Freshly ground black pepper to taste

- Heat the ghee and sauté the garlic, shallots, pandan leaves, star anise, cloves, cardamom and cinnamon for a few minutes until fragrant.

- Add the chicken and then the rice, dhal, peanuts and carrot.

- Pour in the chicken stock, coconut milk and water. Boil until the porridge is cooked, adding more water as required.

- Add the grated coconut, prawns, salt and pepper to taste. Bring to the boil, then remove from heat.

- Garnish with coriander leaves and serve immediately.

NOTE

You may add a 2-cm (1-in) length cinnamon stick, 3 cloves and 4 cardamom pods to the soup while cooking to make it more aromatic, if desired.

VERMICELLI IN SPICED CHICKEN SOUP
SOTO AYAM

Vegetable oil 4 Tbsp + more for frying

Chicken 1, about 1.5 kg (3 lb 4¹⁄₂ oz), cleaned and halved

Water 2 litres (64 fl oz / 8 cups)

Salt to taste

Potatoes 3, large, boiled, peeled and mashed

Minced beef 200 g (7 oz)

Crisp-fried shallots 2 Tbsp + more for garnishing

Grated nutmeg ¹⁄₂ tsp

Clove powder ¹⁄₂ tsp

Spring onions (scallion) 2, finely sliced + more for granishing

Salt to taste

Ground white pepper to taste

Plain (all-purpose) flour 55 g (2 oz)

Egg 1, beaten

Ready-made *nasi himpit* as needed

Dried vermicelli 55 g (2 oz), deep-fried for 5 seconds until it fluffs up

Dark soy sauce to taste

Green bird's eye chilli *(cili padi)* to taste, seeded and pounded finely

Kalamansi limes to taste, halved

Spice paste

Shallots 8, peeled

Garlic 3 cloves, peeled

Coriander powder 1 Tbsp

Lemongrass 2 stalks

Black peppercorns 1 Tbsp

Candlenuts 5

Galangal 1-cm (¹⁄₂-in) knob, peeled

Ginger 1-cm (¹⁄₂-in) knob, peeled

Ground white pepper 1 tsp

Sauce

Chilli sauce to taste

Dark soy sauce 4 Tbsp

Bird's eye chillies *(cili padi)* 6, seeded and pounded

Lime juice 1 Tbsp

Sugar 1 Tbsp

- Combine ingredients for spice paste in a food processor and blend until smooth. Set aside.

- Prepare soup. Heat oil in a wok and fry the spice paste for a few minutes until fragrant. Add the chicken and water and simmer for 1 hour.

- Remove the chicken and season the soup with salt. Shred the chicken meat and set aside.

- Prepare potato cutlet. Combine mashed potatoes with beef, shallots, nutmeg, clove powder, spring onions and ground white pepper. Add salt to taste and mix well.

- Shape into patties. Roll the patties in flour, dip into the egg and fry in hot oil until golden on both sides.

- Combine all ingredients for sauce in a saucepan and simmer for a few minutes. Remove from heat and leave to cool.

- To serve, place *nasi himpit* in individual bowls and pour hot soup over. Garnish with shredded chicken, potato cutlets and fried vermicelli. Serve with a side of dark soy sauce, bird's eye chillies and limes.

VEGETABLE CURRY WITH COCONUT MILK
LONTONG SAYUR LODEH

Cooking oil for shallow-frying

Coconut milk 1 litre (32 fl oz / 4 cups), extracted from 1 grated coconut and 1 litre (32 fl oz / 4 cups) water

Long beans 10, cut into 5-cm (2-in) lengths

Bean curd 3, fried and cut into bite-size pieces

Fermented soy bean cake *(tempe)* 4, fried and cut into bite-size pieces

Aubergine (eggplant/brinjal) 1, cut into 5-cm (2-in) lengths

Cabbage 150 g (5¹/₃ oz), sliced

Yam bean ¹/₂, peeled, sliced and coarsely shredded

Glass noodles 30 g (1 oz), blanched and drained

***Salam* leaves** 4

Kaffir lime leaves 2

Prawns (shrimps) 300 g (10¹/₂ oz), cleaned and shelled

Hard-boiled egg 1, shelled and halved

Spicy meat floss *(serunding) (optional)* as needed

Spice paste

Shallots 10, peeled

Lemongrass 2 stalks, bruised

Ginger 1-cm (¹/₂-in) knob, peeled

Galangal 1 cm (¹/₂-in) knob, peeled

Candlenuts 8

Red chillies 10, seeded

Turmeric 1-cm (¹/₂-in) knob, peeled

Turmeric powder 1 Tbsp

Dried prawn (shrimp) paste *(belacan)* 2 Tbsp

Garlic 4 cloves, peeled

Dried prawns (shrimps) 60 g (2 oz), soaked and drained

- Combine ingredients for spice paste in a food processor and blend until smooth. Heat the oil in a wok and sauté the spice paste until fragrant.
- Add all the remaining ingredients except prawns and hard-boiled eggs and cook until the vegetables soften.
- Add in the prawns and simmer for 10 minutes until the prawns are cooked.
- Serve with egg and spicy meat floss.

LAKSA JOHOR

Vegetable oil 4 Tbsp

Ginger 1-cm (¹/₂-in) knob, peeled and chopped

Shallots 10, peeled and pounded

Garlic 3 cloves, peeled and pounded

Dried prawns (shrimps) 5 Tbsp, soaked, drained and pounded

Fish curry powder 4 heaped Tbsp

Prawns (shrimps) 300 g (10¹/₂ oz), cleaned, shelled and finely minced

Store-bought coconut cream 1 litre (32 fl oz / 4 cups)

Lemongrass 3 stalks, bruised

Galangal 1-cm (¹/₂-in) knob, peeled and bruised

Mackerel fillet 1 kg (2 lb, 3 oz), poached and minced

Dried sour fruit *(asam gelugor)* 5

Pounded roasted grated or desiccated coconut *(kerisik)* 70 g (2¹/₂ oz)

Spaghetti 500 g (1 lb 1¹/₂ oz), cooked

Kalamansi limes 10, halved

Sambal belacan

Red chillies 3, seeded

Dried prawn (shrimp) paste *(belacan)* 1 tsp, toasted

Salt to taste

Lime juice ¹/₂ tsp

Garnish

Cucumber 1, julienned

Laksa **leaves** 8 sprigs, chopped

Bean sprouts 100 g (3¹/₂ oz), tailed

Onions 2, peeled and sliced

Long beans 100 g (3¹/₂ oz), sliced

- Combine ingredients for *sambal belacan* in a food processor and blend until smooth. Set aside.
- Heat the oil in a heavy pot and fry the ginger, shallots, garlic and dried prawns until fragrant. Add the curry powder and fry for 2 minutes.
- Add the prawns, coconut cream, lemongrass and galangal. Leave to simmer.
- Add the mackerel and dried sour fruit and continue to simmer for 20 minutes.
- Add the pounded grated coconut to the stock. Stir and cook for another 2 minutes. If the sauce is too thick, dilute with hot water.
- To serve, divide spaghetti into serving bowls. Garnish with the cucumber, *laksa* leaves, bean sprouts, onions and long beans.
- Pour the sauce over the spaghetti, squeeze some lime on it and serve with *sambal belacan* on the side.

BIBIK NEO'S NYONYA LAKSA
KARI LAKSA BIBIK NEO

Fish cake 1, sliced

Cockles 300 g (10½ oz), soaked in boiling water for 1 minute and flesh removed

Bean sprouts 200 g (7 oz), tailed

Prawns (shrimps) 15, boiled and shelled

Rice vermicelli 300 g (10½ oz), blanched and drained

Cucumber ½, cored and cut into thin strips

Shredded *laksa* leaves 1 Tbsp

Kalamansi limes 10, halved

Gravy

Vegetable oil 180 ml (6 fl oz / ¾ cup)

Coconut milk 250 ml (8 fl oz / 1 cup), extracted from 2 grated coconuts and 250 ml (8 fl oz / 1 cup) water

Water 125 ml (4 fl oz / ½ cup)

Fried bean curd puffs (*taufu pok*) (optional) 10

Fish balls 20

Prawns (shrimps) 500 g (1 lb 1½ oz), shelled, deveined and coarsely chopped

Salt to taste

Sugar to taste

Spice paste for gravy

Shallots 20, peeled

Red chillies 10, seeded

Ground chilli paste 3 Tbsp

Dried prawns (shrimps) 125 g (4½ oz), soaked and drained

Galangal 2-cm (1-in) knob, peeled

Candlenuts 15

Turmeric 3-cm (1½-in) knob, peeled

Kaffir lime leaves 2

Shredded *laksa* leaves 1 Tbsp

Coriander powder 1 Tbsp

- Prepare gravy. Combine ingredients for spice paste in a food processor and blend until smooth.

- Heat the oil in a pot. Fry the spice until fragrant over low heat. Add the coconut milk and water and bring to the boil.

- Add fried bean curd puffs, fish balls, chopped prawns, salt and sugar. Boil until the gravy thickens.

- To serve, place fish cake, cockles, bean sprouts, prawns and noodles into serving bowls and spoon over gravy. Garnish with cucumber, shredded *laksa* leaves and limes. Garnish as desired and serve immediately.

ASAM LAKSA

Thick rice vermicelli 300 g (10^1/$_2$ oz), blanched and drained

Red chillies 2, seeded and thinly sliced

Green chillies 2, seeded and thinly sliced

Torch ginger buds 2, thinly sliced

Laksa **leaves** 15–20, finely sliced

Mint leaves 20

Lettuce 2–3 leaves, finely shredded

Kalamansi limes 6, halved

Pineapple ^{1}/$_2$, peeled and thinly sliced

Hard-boiled egg 1, peeled and quarted

Black prawn (shrimp) paste *(hae ko)* 4 Tbsp

Gravy

Water 500 ml (16 fl oz / 2 cups)

Dried sour fruit *(asam gelugor)* 4 pieces

Laksa **leaves** 15

Torch ginger buds 2, halved lengthwise

Mackerel 1.5 kg (3 lb 4^1/$_2$ oz), cleaned, boiled, deboned and coarsely pounded

Salt to taste

Sugar to taste

Spice paste

Dried chillies 30, soaked in hot water, seeded and drained

Shallots 15, peeled

Garlic 2 cloves, peeled

Dried prawn (shrimp) paste *(belacan)* 1 Tbsp

- Combine ingredients for spice paste in a food processor and blend until smooth.

- Prepare gravy. Put the spice paste, water, dried sour fruit, *laksa* leaves, torch ginger buds and fish into a pot. Bring to the boil and season with salt and sugar. Allow gravy to simmer until it thickens slightly.

- To serve, place vermicelli into bowls and pour gravy over. Top with the remaining ingredients and serve immediately.

MUM'S MEE BANDUNG
MI BANDUNG EMAK

Cooking oil for shallow- or deep-frying

Firm bean curd 1 piece

Eggs 2

Shallots 3, peeled and sliced

Garlic 4 cloves, peeled and minced

Ginger 2-cm (1-in) knob, peeled and minced

Ground chilli paste 2 Tbsp

Chicken stock (see Note on page 70) 500 ml (16 fl oz / 2 cups)

Prawns (shrimps) 200 g (7 oz) shelled and deveined

Squid tubes 200 g (7 oz), cut as desired

Tomato sauce 125 ml (4 fl oz / ½ cup)

Thai roasted chilli paste *(nam prik phao)* 2 Tbsp

Cabbage 100 g (3½ oz), shredded

Chinese flowering cabbage *(chye sim)* 3 stalks, cut into 3-cm (1½-in) lengths

Fish balls 6

Bean sprouts a handful, tailed, if desired

Fresh yellow noodles 200 g (7 oz) blanched and drained

Salt to taste

Crisp-fried shallots as needed

Red chillies 2–3, seeded and sliced

Green chillies 2, seeded and sliced

Spring onions (scallions) (optional) 2–3, diagonally sliced

Coriander leaves (cilantro) (optional) a handful, chopped

- Heat sufficient oil for shallow- or deep-frying in a wok. Add bean curd and fry until golden brown. Remove and drain on paper towels. Cool and cut bean curd into small cubes.

- Remove excess oil from pan, leaving about 4 Tbsp behind. Reheat oil and fry each egg sunny-side up. Remove and set aside.

- Assess oil left in the pan and add sufficient oil to have about 4 Tbsp inside. Reheat oil and fry shallots, garlic and ginger until fragrant. Add ground chilli paste and fry for 1 minute.

- Add chicken stock, prawns, squid, tomato sauce and Thai roasted chilli paste. Stir through, then add cabbage, Chinese flowering cabbage, fish balls, bean sprouts, noodles and fried bean curd. Stir until well combined and season to taste with salt.

- When prawns and squid are cooked, turn off heat. Transfer to individual serving bowls and top with fried eggs. Garnish with crisp-fried shallots and chillies. Serve immediately.

CIK ANI'S MEE REBUS
MI REBUS CIK AINI

Fresh yellow noodles 2 kg (4 lb 6 oz), blanched just before serving

Bean sprouts 200 g (7 oz), blanched just before serving

Firm bean curd 4 pieces, deep-fried and cut into 6 pieces each

Green chillies 3, seeded and sliced

Red chillies 2, seeded and sliced

Chinese celery 4 sprigs, sliced

Spring onions (scallions) 4, sliced

Crisp-fried shallots 55 g (2 oz)

Hard-boiled eggs 3, shelled and cut into wedges

Kalamansi limes 6, halved

Gravy

Cooking oil 4 Tbsp

Meat curry powder 3 Tbsp

Preserved soy bean paste *(tau cheo)* 110 g (4 oz)

Beef 1 kg (2 lb 3 oz), cut into small pieces

Water as needed

Sweet potatoes 1 kg (2 lb 3 oz), boiled, peeled and mashed

Galangal 2-cm (1-in) knob, peeled and bruised

Tomatoes 5, quartered

Peanuts 85 g (3 oz), roasted and pounded

Salt to taste

Sugar to taste

Spice paste

Shallots 10, peeled

Garlic 6 cloves, peeled

Ginger 1-cm ($\frac{1}{2}$-in) knob, peeled

- Make gravy. Combine ingredients for spice paste in a food processor and blend until smooth.

- Heat oil in a wok and sauté spice paste until fragrant. Add meat curry powder and preserved soy bean paste and sauté until fragrant.

- Add beef, water, sweet potatoes and galangal and boil for 20 minutes.

- Add tomatoes and peanuts and lower heat to simmer until tomatoes are soft. Season with salt and sugar. Set aside.

- Put noodles in individual serving bowls and top with bean sprouts. Pour gravy over and garnish with fried bean curd, chillies, Chinese celery, spring onions, crisp-fried shallots, eggs and limes. Serve immediately.

SARAWAK LAKSA

Vegetable oil 250 ml (8 fl oz / 1 cup)

Chicken ¹/₂, about 500 g (1 lb 1¹/₂ oz), cleaned

Prawn (shrimp) stock (see page 254) 500 ml (16 fl oz / 2 cups)

Coconut milk 1 litre (32 fl oz / 4 cups), extracted from 2 grated coconuts and 1 litre (32 fl oz / 4 cups) water

Salt to taste

Sugar to taste

Medium prawns (shrimps) 1 kg (2 lb 3 oz), cleaned and shelled

Rice vermicelli 300 g (10¹/₂ oz), soaked, blanched and drained

Coriander leaves (cilantro) 200 g (7 oz), shredded

Bean sprouts 300 g (10¹/₂ oz), tailed and blanched

Cucumbers 2, peeled, cored and shredded

Crisp-fried shallots 125 g (4¹/₂ oz)

Hard-boiled eggs 3, shelled and sliced

Red chilli 1, seeded and sliced

Mint leaves a bunch, shredded

Kalamansi limes 3, halved

Bottled *sambal belacan* **(optional)** as needed

Spice paste

Shallots 30, peeled

Garlic 4 cloves, peeled

Dried chillies 30, soaked, seeded and drained

Dried prawns (shrimps) 200 g (7 oz), soaked and drained

Candlenuts 10

Black peppercorns 10

Ginger 2-cm (1-in) knob, peeled

Coriander powder 3 Tbsp

Cumin powder 1 Tbsp

Lemongrass 3 stalks, thinly sliced

Galangal 2.5-cm (1-in) knob, peeled

- Combine ingredients for spice paste in a food processor and blend until smooth.

- Heat oil in a pot over medium heat and sauté the spice paste until fragrant.

- Put in the chicken, prawn stock and coconut milk. Bring to the boil, then lower heat and simmer until the chicken is tender, about 45 minutes. Season with salt and sugar. Remove the chicken.

- Allow the chicken to cool before shredding the meat. Set aside.

- In the meantime, put the prawns into the soup and cook for 5 minutes. Remove the prawns and set aside.

- To serve, place some noodles into a bowl and pour over gravy. Top with shredded chicken, prawns, coriander leaves, bean sprouts, cucumber, crisp-fried shallots, egg, chillies, mint leaves and limes. Serve with *sambal belacan*, if desired.

PRAWN MEE
MI UDANG

Medium-size prawns (shrimps) 1 kg (2 lb 3 oz), cleaned and shelled, shells reserved to make stock

Vegetable oil 125 ml (4 fl oz / 1/2 cup)

Chicken carcass 2, cleaned

Tientsin cabbage 100 g (3 1/2 oz)

Water 2 litres (64 fl oz / 8 cups)

Ground white pepper 2 tsp

Salt to taste

Sugar to taste

Yellow noodles 300 g (10 1/2 oz)

Chicken breasts 3, about 140 g (5 oz) each, boiled and shredded

Bean sprouts 100 g (3 1/2 oz), tailed and blanched

Water convolvulus 55 g (2 oz), plucked and blanched

Hard-boiled eggs 4, shelled and halved

Crisp-fried shallots 200 g (7 oz)

Pounded ingredients

Shallots 15, peeled

Garlic 4 cloves, peeled

Dried shrimps 100 g (3 1/2 oz), soaked and drained

Preserved soy bean paste *(tau cheo)* 2 Tbsp

Sweet sambal

Cooking oil 4 Tbsp

Dried chillies 25, soaked, seeded, drained and ground to a paste

Shallots 8, peeled and ground

Dried prawn (shrimp) paste *(belacan)* 2 tsp, ground

Sugar 6 Tbsp

- Prepare sweet *sambal*. Heat the oil in a wok and fry the ground ingredients until fragrant. Then add sugar and stir-fry for a couple of minutes. Set aside.

- Cook the prawns in boiling water. Drain and reserve the stock.

- Heat oil in a pot. Fry the pounded ingredients until fragrant. Put in the prawns shells and fry for another 5 minutes or until fragrant.

- Put in the chicken carcasses, Tientsin cabbage, water, prawn stock and simmer for 30 minutes. Add 250 ml (8 fl oz / 1 cup) water if necessary. Add pepper, salt and sugar to taste.

- Once the soup is flavourful, remove shells and carcasses and strain.

- To serve, place some noodles, cooked prawns, shredded chicken, bean sprouts, water convolvulus and egg in a bowl. Pour hot soup over and garnish with crisp-fried shallots. Serve with prepared sweet *sambal* on the side.

FLAT RICE NOODLES WITH FISH BALLS

SUP KWAY TEOW

Chicken stock (see Note on page 70)
2.5 litres (80 fl oz / 10 cups)

Anchovies *(ikan bilis)* 10–20 g, cleaned

Tientsin cabbage 4 Tbsp

Ground white pepper 2 tsp

Fish balls 30

Fresh flat rice noodles 300 g (10½ oz),
blanched and drained

Light soy sauce 4 Tbsp

Bird's eye chillies *(cili padi)* 3, seeded and
thinly sliced

Garnishing

Fish cakes 2, sliced

Dried bean curd skin *(foo pei)* 1, halved

Crisp-fried shallots to sprinkle

Spring onion (scallion) 1, finely sliced

Bean sprouts 55 g (2 oz), tailed and
blanched

- Put the chicken stock, anchovies, Tientsin cabbage and pepper into a pot and bring to the boil. Simmer for 20 minutes, adding water if necessary.

- Put in the fish balls and cook until they rise to the surface.

- To serve, place rice noodles, fish cake slices and dried bean curd skin into a bowl. Spoon some fish balls and soup over the ingredients. Sprinkle with crisp-fried shallots, spring onion and bean sprouts. Serve with light soy sauce and sliced chillies on the side.

HOKKIEN MEE
MI HOKKIEN

Cooking oil 4 Tbsp

Garlic 3 cloves, peeled and minced

Ginger 1-cm (½-in) knob, peeled and minced

Squid 200 g (7 oz), cleaned and sliced

Prawns (shrimps) 200 g (7 oz), cleaned and shelled

Chicken thigh or breast meat 200 g (7 oz), sliced and seasoned with light soy sauce and corn flour (cornstarch)

Chinese flowering cabbage *(chye sim)* 55 g, (2 oz) washed and plucked

Oyster sauce 1 Tbsp

Dark soy sauce 1½ Tbsp

Light soy sauce 1 Tbsp

Sesame oil ½ Tbsp

Fresh yellow noodles 350 g (12 oz), washed

Salt to taste

Sugar to taste

- Heat oil in a wok and stir-fry the garlic and ginger until fragrant.

- Add the squid, prawns and chicken and stir-fry for a few minutes. Remove the squid when cooked.

- Add the remaining ingredients to the wok and stir-fry for another 3–4 minutes. Return squid to the wok. Season with salt and sugar and serve immediately.

CURRY NOODLES
MI KARI

Cooking oil for shallow- or deep-frying

Fried bean curd puffs *(taufu pok)* 2 pieces

Cinnamon stick 3-cm (1¹/₂-in)

Cloves 3

Star anise 1

Cardamom pods 3

Meat curry powder 45 g (1¹/₂ oz) mixed into a paste with a little water

Curry leaves 3 sprigs

Chicken breast or thigh meat 250 g (9 oz) cut into bite-size pieces

Prawns (shrimps) 150 g (5¹/₃ oz), cleaned and shelled with tails intact

Ready-made chicken meatballs 200 g (7 oz), halved

Dried sour fruit *(asam gelugor)* 2–3 pieces or more to taste

Coconut milk 500 ml (16 fl oz / 2 cups), extracted from 1 grated coconut and 500 ml (16 fl oz / 2 cups) water

Water 625 ml (20 fl oz / 2¹/₂ cups)

Salt ¹/₂ tsp or to taste

Tomatoes 2, cut into small wedges

Fresh yellow noodles 350 g (11¹/₂ oz), blanched and drained

Bean sprouts 200 g (7 oz), tailed and blanched

Chinese flowering cabbage *(chye sim)* 600 g (1 lb 5 oz), blanched and cut into bite-size pieces

Coriander leaves (cilantro) 3 sprigs, coarsely chopped

Spice paste

Shallots 3, peeled

Garlic 2 cloves, peeled

Ginger 2-cm (1-in) knob, peeled and sliced

- Combine all ingredients for spice paste in a food processor and blend until smooth. Set aside.

- Heat sufficient oil for shallow- or deep-frying in a wok. Add bean curd puffs and fry until golden brown. Remove and drain on paper towels. Once cool, cut bean curd into small cubes.

- Remove excess oil from the pan, leaving about 2 Tbsp behind. Reheat oil and fry spice paste, cinnamon, cloves, star anise and cardamom pods over low heat until lightly browned. Add curry paste and curry leaves. Stir until fragrant.

- Add chicken pieces and stir until they are well coated with curry mixture. Sprinkle in some water, cover and cook over medium heat for about 5 minutes.

- Add prawns, chicken meatballs, dried sour fruit, coconut milk and water. Stir through and simmer for 5 minutes, then season to taste with salt. Cook for 3–4 minutes more before adding tomatoes. Stir through and remove from heat.

- To serve, put some noodles, bean sprouts, Chinese flowering cabbage and fried bean curd puffs into individual serving bowls, then ladle hot gravy. Sprinkle with coriander and serve immediately.

FRIED YELLOW NOODLES
MI GORENG

Prawns (shrimps) 200 g (7 oz), cleaned and shelled, shells reserved to make stock

Water 180 ml (6 fl oz / ¾ cup)

Vegetable oil 4 Tbsp

Garlic 2 cloves, peeled and minced

Ground chilli paste 1 Tbsp

Thick sweet soy sauce 1 Tbsp

Oyster sauce 2 Tbsp

Tomato sauce 4 Tbsp

Chicken breast or thigh meat 200 g (7 oz)

Green mustard leaves 200 g (7 oz), chopped

Fresh yellow noodles 500 g (1 lb 1½ oz)

Salt to taste

Sugar to taste

Bean sprouts 100 g (3½ oz)

Firm bean curd 1 piece, fried and sliced

Tomato 1, quartered

Kalamansi limes 4, halved

Crisp-fried shallots 125 g (4½ oz)

Spring onions (scallions) 2, finely chopped

- To make prawn stock, simmer prawn shells in water for 30 minutes. Remove from heat, strain and set aside.

- Heat the oil in a wok and brown garlic. Add chilli paste and fry until fragrant. Add thick soy sauce, oyster sauce and tomato sauce.

- Stir in prawns and chicken and leave to cook for a few minutes.

- Add the mustard leaves and noodles and season with salt and sugar. Stir the noodles quickly. Then add stock, bean sprouts, bean curd and tomato.

- Fry for 2 minutes and garnish with limes, fried shallots and spring onions. Serve immediately.

FRIED VERMICELLI
BIHUN GORENG

Vegetable oil 4 Tbsp

Garlic 4 cloves, peeled and minced

Ground chilli paste 3 Tbsp

Dried prawns (shrimps) 55 g (2 oz), soaked, drained and pounded

Preserved soy bean paste *(tau cheo)* 3 Tbsp

Prawns (shrimps) 300 g (10^1/$_2$ oz), cleaned and shelled

Cockles 100 g (3^1/$_2$ oz), soaked in boiling water for 1 minute and flesh removed

Fish balls or fish cake 100 g (3^1/$_2$ oz), thinly sliced

Chinese chives 5 stalks

Green mustard leaves 100 g (3^1/$_2$ oz), chopped

Dried rice vermicelli 300 g (10^1/$_2$ oz), soaked

Coriander leaves (cilantro) 55 g (2 oz), thinly sliced

Bean sprouts 100 g (3^1/$_2$ oz), tailed

Salt to taste

Ground white pepper to taste

Eggs 3, made into an omelette and cut into strips

Red chillies 3, seeded and sliced

- Heat oil in a wok and fry the garlic, chilli paste and dried prawns until fragrant.

- Add preserved soy bean paste, prawns, cockles, fish balls or fish cake, Chinese chives and green mustard leaves.

- Stir in the vermicelli, coriander leaves and bean sprouts. Season with salt and pepper.

- Garnish with egg and chillies and serve immediately.

FRIED TOM YAM VERMICELLI

BIHUN GORENG TOM YAM

Cooking oil 1 Tbsp + more for shallow-frying

Chicken breast or thigh meat 300 g (10½ oz), sliced into bite-size pieces

Firm bean curd 3 pieces, cut into bite-size pieces

Oyster sauce 4 Tbsp

Fish sauce 4 Tbsp

Preserved soy bean paste *(tau cheo)* 2 Tbsp

Sugar to taste

Dried rice vermicelli 500 g (1 lb 1½ oz), blanched and drained

Chinese chives 10 stalks, sliced

Bean sprouts 200 g (7 oz), tailed if desired and rinsed clean

Fish cakes (optional) 2 pieces, cooked and sliced thinly

Red chilli 1, seeded and sliced

Spice paste

Dried chillies 15 soaked, seeded and drained

Lemongrass 1 stalk, sliced

Ginger 1-cm (½-in) knob, peeled and sliced

Galangal 1-cm (½-in) knob, peeled and sliced

Dried prawns (shrimps) 70 g (2½ oz), rinsed clean, soaked in water to soften and drained

Dried prawn (shrimp) paste *(belacan)* 2 tsp, toasted

Coriander leaves (cilantro) 5 sprigs

Kaffir lime leaves 2, shredded

Garlic 3 cloves, peeled

Shallots 8, peeled

- Combine ingredients for spice paste in a food processor and blend until smooth. Set aside.

- Heat 1 Tbsp oil in a wok. Fry chicken until lightly browned. Remove and set aside.

- Add sufficient oil to wok for shallow-frying and reheat. Fry bean curd pieces until golden brown, then remove and drain on paper towels.

- Assess oil left in the wok and either add or remove oil to have about 4 Tbsp inside. Reheat oil and fry spice paste until fragrant. Add oyster sauce, fish sauce, preserved soy bean paste and sugar. Stir well.

- Add vermicelli and a little water. Toss until vermicelli is well combined with other ingredients. While stir-frying, it may be necessary to keep adding small amounts of water to prevent the vermicelli from drying out; at no point should the vermicelli be hard and brittle.

- Add fried bean curd and chicken, chives, bean sprouts and fish cakes (if using) to the wok. Stir-fry until well combined, then turn off heat. Dish out onto serving plate. Garnish with chilli and serve immediately.

FRIED FLAT RICE NOODLES
KWAY TEOW GORENG

Vegetable oil 3 Tbsp

Garlic 2 cloves, peeled and minced

Ground chilli paste 1 Tbsp

Dark soy sauce 2 Tbsp

Oyster sauce 2 Tbsp

Prawns (shrimps) 200 g (7 oz), cleaned and shelled

Cockles (optional) 100 g (3¹/₂ oz), soaked in boiling water for 1 minute and flesh removed

Flat rice noodles 400 g (14 oz)

Chinese chives 55 g (2 oz), sliced

Bean sprouts 100 g (3¹/₂ oz), tailed

Firm bean curd 1 piece, fried and cubed

Water 4 Tbsp

- Heat oil in a wok and fry the garlic until golden brown.

- Add the chilli paste and fry until fragrant.

- Add dark soy sauce and oyster sauce and stir through. Then add the prawns, cockles (if using) and noodles and stir-fry for a few minutes.

- Add the chives, bean sprouts and bean curd. Sprinkle over some water and stir for a few minutes. Serve immediately.

SOUPS

CHEF WAN'S OXTAIL SOUP
SUP EKOR CHEF WAN

Vegetable oil 125 ml (4 fl oz / ½ cup)

Oxtail 500 g (1 lb 1½ oz), cleaned and cut into bite-size pieces

Coriander powder 2 Tbsp

Cumin powder 1 Tbsp

Fennel powder 1 Tbsp

Tomato purée 1½ Tbsp

Water 1.5 litres (48 fl oz / 6 cups)

Carrot 1, peeled and sliced

Potato 1, peeled and cut into quarters

Celery 2 stalks, diced

Salt to taste

Freshly ground black pepper to taste

Spring onions (scallions) as needed, chopped

Crisp-fried shallots as needed

Whole spices

Cardamom pods 4

Cinnamon stick 1-cm (½-in)

Cloves 6

Star anise 2

Spice paste

Shallots 10, peeled

Garlic 4 cloves, peeled

Lemongrass 2 stalks, finely sliced

Ginger 1-cm (½-in) knob, peeled

- Combine ingredients for spice paste in a food processor and blend until smooth. Set aside.

- Heat the oil in a large pot and sear the oxtail until slightly browned. Drain and set aside.

- In the same pot, sauté the whole spices and spice paste until fragrant. Add the coriander, cumin and fennel powders and sauté over low heat for 3–4 minutes until fragrant.

- Add the tomato purée, oxtail and water and bring to a simmer.

- Add the carrot, potato and celery. Simmer over medium heat for 1 hour 45 minutes until the oxtail is tender.

- Season with salt and pepper. Just before serving, garnish with spring onions and crisp-fried shallots.

MUTTON SOUP
SUP KAMBING

Cooking oil 4 Tbsp

Onions 2, peeled and thinly sliced

Cinnamon stick 2-cm (1-in)

Cardamom pods 6

Cloves 10

Star anise 4

Coriander powder 3 Tbsp

Fennel powder 2 Tbsp

Cumin powder 2 Tbsp

Ground white pepper 1 Tbsp

Mutton 1 kg (2 lb 3 oz), with bones

Carrots 2, peeled and cut into chunks

Celery 3 stalks, sliced

Potatoes 4, peeled and quartered

Water 1.5 litres (48 fl oz / 6 cups)

Salt to taste

Coriander leaves (cilantro) 20 sprigs, finely chopped

Spring onions (scallions) 5, finely sliced

Spice paste

Lemongrass 4 stalks

Galangal 2-cm (1-in) knob, peeled

Shallots 15, peeled

Garlic 4 cloves, peeled

Black peppercorns 4 Tbsp

Ginger 3-cm (1½-in) knob, peeled

- Combine ingredients for spice paste in a food processor and blend until smooth. Set aside.

- Heat oil in a wok. Fry the onions, cinnamon, cardamoms, cloves and star anise until fragrant.

- Add the prepared spice paste, coriander, fennel and cumin powders and pepper to the wok. Cook over low heat until fragrant and the oil surfaces.

- Put in the mutton, carrots, celery, potatoes and water. Bring to the boil and simmer for at least 1 hour or until the meat is tender. If necessary, add more water from time to time to ensure there is enough liquid for the meat to cook and become tender. Add salt to taste. Garnish with coriander leaves and spring onions before serving.

YONG TOW FOO

Deep-fried firm bean curd pieces 2

Ladies fingers *(okra)* 3, slit lengthwise

Bittergourd ¹/₂, sliced and pith removed

Aubergine (eggplant/brinjal) 1

Red chillies 4, seeded and slit lengthwise

Fish balls 6

Fish paste

Mackerel 500 g (1 lb 1¹/₂ oz), skinned, deboned and minced into a smooth paste

Tapioca flour 1 tsp

Ground white pepper ¹/₂ tsp

Salt ¹/₂ tsp

Soup

Garlic 2 cloves, peeled and finely minced

Anchovies (*ikan bilis*) 55 g (2 oz), pounded

Water 1 litre (32 fl oz / 4 cups)

Anchovy *(ikan bilis)* stock granules 1 tsp

- Cut firm bean curd pieces into triangles and make a small insertion, removing a small portion of the bean curd in the centre to create a small pocket. Slice aubergine into thick rounds and slice each round lengthwise making sure not to slice all the way through.

- Combine ingredients for fish paste in a bowl and mix well. Then take the fish paste, a little at a time, and slap the paste against the bowl about 15 times. This process will help the paste take on a spongy texture.

- Stuff bean curd and vegetables with fish paste.

- Place ingredients for soup in a large pot and bring to the boil. Add stuffed bean curd, vegetables and fish balls and simmer for 10 minutes.

- Remove from heat. Serve hot with a side of *hoisin* sauce and chilli sauce.

BEAN CURD SOUP
SUP TAUHU

Cooking oil 1 Tbsp

Onions 4, peeled and sliced

Medium prawns (shrimps) 150 g (5¹/₃ oz), cleaned and shelled, shells reserved to make stock

Prawn (shrimp) stock (see page 254) 500 ml (16 fl oz / 2 cups)

Freshly ground black pepper a pinch

Silken bean curd 1 block, about 250 g (9 oz), cut into cubes

Salt to taste

Sugar to taste

Chopped coriander leaves (cilantro) for garnishing

- Heat oil in a wok and fry the onions until fragrant.
- Add in the prawns until prawns turn pink. Add in the stock and pepper.
- Let it boil for about 5 minutes, then add in the bean curd.
- Simmer for about 1 minute and season with salt and sugar. Garnish with coriander leaves and serve immediately.

CHICKEN SOUP
SUP AYAM

Vegetable oil 6 Tbsp

Cinnamon stick 2.5-cm (1-in)

Cardamom pods 6

Cloves 3

Star anise 2

Chicken 1, about 1.5 kg (3 lb 4¹/₂ oz),
cut into bite-size pieces

Water 1.5 litres (48 fl oz / 6 cups)

Carrot 1, large, peeled and cut into 5-cm
(2-in) lengths

Potatoes 2, peeled and quartered

Salt to taste

Ground white pepper to taste

Spring onion (scallion) 1, chopped

Coriander leaves (cilantro) 2 sprigs,
chopped

Crisp-fried shallots 125 g (4¹/₂ oz)

Spice paste

Shallots 10, peeled

Ginger 2-cm (³/₄-in) knob, peeled

Garlic 2 cloves, peeled

Black peppercorns 1 Tbsp

Coriander seeds 2 Tbsp

Cumin seeds 1 Tbsp

Fennel seeds 1 Tbsp

- Combine ingredients for spice paste in a food processor and blend until smooth.

- Heat oil in a wok and fry the spice paste for a few minutes until fragrant.

- Add the cinnamon stick, cardamom pods, cloves, star anise and chicken. Stir-fry the mixture for about 5 minutes.

- Add water, carrot and potatoes and simmer for 1 hour.

- Season with salt and pepper. Sprinkle over with spring onions, coriander leaves and crisp-fried shallots and serve immediately.

GLOSSARY

Bamboo shoots

Banana flower

Bay leaves

Fried bean curd puffs

Candlenuts

Cardamom pods

Chillies

Chinese chives

Cinnamon

Bamboo shoots The tender, young shoots of the bamboo are harvested when they first appear at the base of the bamboo plant. The bamboo shoot is covered with dark coloured leaves, which should first be peeled off before use. Inside, the flesh is cream-coloured. Fresh bamboo shoots must be boiled for at least 1 hour before it is ready for use. After boiling, leave the shoots to soak in water until required. Bamboo shoots are available fresh, canned or pickled.

Banana flower Known as *jantung pisang* to Malay-speakers, this deep-red flower consists of tightly packed leaves that wrap around the rows of thin-stemmed flowers. The flowers need to be steamed for about 20 minutes before used in cooking. In Southeast Asian cooking, banana flowers are sliced and cooked in curries, soups and stir-fries.

Bay leaves Available fresh or dried, bay leaves impart a pleasant aroma to dishes such as curry, stews and soups in Asian cooking. Although fresh bay leaves have a stronger aroma, the readily-available dried version is more commonly used.

Bean curd Bean curd or soy bean cake is made from ground soy beans. High in protein and low in calories, it comes in several forms: fresh, dried and pickled. Fresh bean curd has a delicate flavour not found in either the dried or the pickled form.

Firm bean curd comes in pieces about 6–8-cm (2^1/$_2$–3-in) squares. It is usually used for stuffing or is braised, stewed or deep-fried.

Silken bean curd is mainly steamed, scrambled or used in soups.

Dried bean curd sheets, which are sold in large pieces that need to be wiped with a damp cloth to clean and soften, are used as wrappers.

Candlenuts Known to Malay-speakers as *buah keras*, candlenuts are hard, yellow, waxy and largely tasteless. They are generally the size of a shelled walnut and are typically pounded and added to curries to thicken them. If unavailable, use macadamia, brazil or cashew nuts instead. Substitute 1 macadamia nut for 1 candlenut; 1 brazil nut for 2–3 candlenuts; and 2 cashew nuts for 1 candlenut.

Cardamom pods Cardamom is the world's most expensive spice after saffron. Cardamom pods are the dried fruit of a perennial plant of the ginger family indigenous to Sri Lanka and south India. The pale green oval pods, which are the best variety, contain 15–20 brown or black seeds. The white pods are simply green pods that have been bleached in the sun.

Chillies Chillies, both red and green, are used extensively in many Asian cuisines. Generally, the larger the chilli, the milder it is. Of the larger chillies, the red ones taste somewhat sweeter than the green ones. Bird's eye chillies, or *cili padi* (pictured), are rarely longer than 5-cm (2-in) and are especially fiery. Both red and green bird's eye chillies pack a punch.

Chinese chives Also known as garlic chives or flat chives, Chinese chives are milder than the dark green variety. They are used to flavour and garnish dishes.

Cinnamon Cinnamon, the edible bark of a tree native to Sri Lanka, is probably the most popular cooking spice in the Western world. The innermost layer of the bark is sold as thin, fragile quills in India (*darchini*), Sri Lanka (*kurundu*), Indonesia (*kayu manis*) and Malaysia and Singapore (*kulit kayu manis*) and is used for flavouring meat, poultry and desserts. The spice is also available powdered, but its flavour and aroma dissipate rather quickly in this form.

Cloves

Coconut milk

Coconut snails

Coriander leaves

Coriander powder

Cumin powder

Curry leaves

**Dried prawn (shrimp) paste
(*belacan*)**

Dried prawns (shrimps)

Cloves Cloves, known as *bunga cengkih* to Malay-speakers, are actually the flower buds of a tree of the myrtle family indigenous to the Maluku Islands (Moluccas) or the Spice Islands. The buds are harvested and dried under the sun for days. Cloves have a stronger flavour than most other spices and are therefore used in smaller quantities.

Coconut milk Coconut milk is not the water found in the middle of the coconut; rather it is the liquid extracted from soaking fresh grated coconut in water and then straining it. There are two types of coconut milk: thick coconut milk comes from the first squeeze of grated coconut with a small amount of water, while thin coconut milk is obtained from the second squeeze with considerably more water.

Coconut snails These spiral-shaped sea snails are known as *siput hisap* to Malay-speakers. It is also sometimes known as *balitung* in Malaysia and Singapore. In Southeast Asian cooking, these molluscs are commonly served stir-fried with chilli or added to curries. They are cooked with the shells intact. The meat is extracted by sucking at the wider end of the shell.

Coriander leaves (cilantro) Also known as cilantro or Chinese parsley, coriander is indigenous to southern Europe. All parts of the plant can be used, even the roots, which are an essential ingredients in Thai cooking. Coriander leaves are used to flavour and garnish dishes.

Coriander powder This is made from pounded coriander seeds, which are really the dried fruit of the coriander plant (*Coriandrum sativum*). Coriander powder and coriander seeds form the backbone of many Indian curries.

Cumin powder Cumin powder is derived from pounded cumin seeds. Like coriander, these small, rice-like grains are called seeds even though they are actually the dried fruit of a plant (*Cuminum cyminum*) that belongs to the parsley family. Cumin, which Malay-speakers known as *jintan putih*, is a key ingredient in ready-made curry powders and is very pungent. Whether whole or ground, use it sparingly.

Curry leaves True to their name, curry leaves give off the distinctive aroma of curry and impart an inimitable peppery flavour to dishes. The plant from which these fragrant leaves grow (*Murraya koenigii*) is native to South Asia.

Dried prawn (shrimp) paste (belacan) Dried prawn paste is typically sold in the form of rectangular blocks. Be warned that its pungent fishy smell intensifies with dry-roasting, which is often necessary before use. When it has been mixed with some pounded chillies and lime juice, however, the transformation is remarkable. The dried prawn paste becomes an enticing flavouring agent and the mixture makes a great side dip, known as *sambal belacan* in Malaysia and Singapore. The paste is often also added in small quantities to stir-fried dishes and thick, curried stews.

Dried prawns (shrimps) Dried prawns are boiled or steamed and then shelled and dried. The best dried prawns are a deep salmon pink. They should not be hard or smell strongly of ammonia. Dried prawns are used—either whole or pounded—in several Asian cuisines, both as a flavouring agent and as the main ingredient.

Dried sour fruit

Fennel powder

Fermented durian

Fermented soy bean cake

Fiddlehead fern

Four-angled beans

Fresh yellow noodles

Galangal

Ginger

Dried sour fruit The ingredient has no common English name, and dried sour fruit is a direct translation of *asam gelugor*, its Malay name. When looking for them in the supermarket or shops, be mindful that many suppliers are known to mislabel them as 'tamarind pieces' or 'tamarind skins' even though the plant from which this fruit is derived is completely unrelated to the tamarind family. These dried slices are added only to liquid-based dishes and, like tamarind, impart sourness to the dish. The longer they have been cooked in the dish, the more sour the dish becomes, so remove them according to taste.

Fennel powder Also known as sweet cumin or *jintan manis* to Malay-speakers, fennel seeds are pungent and only small quantities are required to impart a sweet fragrance and flavour that is strongly reminiscent of aniseed or liquorice to the dish.

Fermented durian Known as *tempoyak* in Malaysia and Indonesia, fermented durian is usually derived from lower quality durian unsuitable for immediate consumption. It is typically added to curries as a flavouring agent.

Fermented soy bean cake Fermented soy bean cake, more commonly known as *tempe* in Southeast Asia, is used a lot in Malaysian and Indonesian cooking. The soy beans are soaked overnight, hulled and steamed for 30 minutes, soaked overnight again, inoculated with a pure culture of *Rhizopus oligosporu*, wrapped in large leaves and set aside for 24 hours.

Fiddlehead ferns These jade green ferns are known as *pucuk paku* in Malaysia and Indonesia. The tips are blanched and put in salads or stir-fried quickly to retain its crunchiness.

Four-angled beans Other names for the four-angled bean are asparagus bean, asparagus pea, winged bean, frilly bean, manilla bean, Goa bean, Mauritius bean and princess pea. In Malaysia, it is known as *kacang botol*. The pods of the bean are very decorative, with four serrated edges and tiny seeds contained inside a central rib' They are generally green, but they may also be pink, purple or red. In Asian cooking, four-angled beans are usually stir-fried or added to salads.

Fresh yellow noodles Fresh yellow noodles are made from flour and eggs and are used mainly in Hokkien dishes. However, Malay and Indian cooks use these noodles for *mee rebus* and *mee goreng*. Spaghetti is a good substitute if fresh yellow noodles are unavailable.

Galangal Galangal, known as *lengkuas* to Malay-speakers, is native to Malaysia and Indonesia. It has a delicate flavour and is normally used fresh in Malaysian, Indonesian and Thai cooking. When the fresh variety is unavailable, dried or powdered galangal can be used instead. In a recipe, 1 Tbsp chopped fresh galangal is equivalent to 1 tsp powdered galangal.

Ginger This fleshy rhizome is used in the West to make gingerbread, ginger beer, candied ginger and chocolate ginger. Fresh ginger is a basic ingredient in many Asian cuisines. It is usually sliced, finely chopped, pounded or ground and used in savoury dishes. Sometimes the juice is extracted and used.

Glass noodles

Ground chilli paste

Kaffir lime leaves

Kalamansi limes

Laksa leaves

Lemongrass

Limes

Mustard seeds

Oyster sauce

Glass noodles The vermicelli-like glass noodles are made from mung bean flour. They are also called cellophane noodles or bean starch noodles. They should be soaked in water before being added to boiling soups or stir-fried vegetables. Glass noodles are used in Japanese, Thai, Burmese, Vietnamese, Chinese, Malaysian, Filipino and Indonesian cooking.

Ground chilli paste Known as *cili boh* in Malaysia and Singapore, this chilli paste is made by blending softened dried chillies with water. Ready-made ground chilli paste is available at supermarkets. To make, wash, seed and soak about 12 dried chillies. Place softened chillies in a food processor with 3–4 Tbsp water and blend until smooth.

Kaffir lime leaves Kaffir lime leaves, or *daun limau purut* to Malay-speakers, are sometimes known as double lime leaves because of the way they grow on branches. Typically added to liquid-based dishes, such as curries, stews or soups, the leaves are tough and fibrous and can be unpleasant to eat. This is why they are usually used whole but bruised or torn to release their fragrance. Alternatively, they can be finely shredded after removing the central stems.

Kalamansi limes A small variety of lime, the kalamansi or musk lime is 2–3-cm (1–1 1/2-in) in diameter. Green or greenish yellow in colour, it is more fragrant than the lime. Kalamansi are generally used to flavour Southeast Asian curries, *sambals* and noodle soups. If unavailable, they may be substituted with half-ripe kumquats or even lemons.

Laksa leaves This narrow, pointed leaf is an essential ingredient in the famous Singaporean/Malaysian seafood noodle soup, *laksa*. They are also known as *daun kesum*. In Vietnam, where they are called *rau ram*, they are used in salads or eaten fresh with the popular *cha gio*.

Lemongrass Lemongrass, a long lemon-scented grass, is popular for flavouring curries and soups in Southeast Asian cuisine. Only the pale lower portion of the stem, with the tough outer layers peeled away, is used for cooking. If lemongrass is unavailable, 2–3 strips of thinly peeled lemon zest can be used as a substitute.

Limes Several varieties of limes are sold throughout Southeast Asia. Among them is the common lime (pictured), which Malay-speakers know as *limau nipis*, and a smaller, far more fragrant variety known as kalamansi limes, which Malay-speakers call *limau kasturi*. Another type, the kaffir or Thai lime, has thick and knobbly skin. It does not yield much juice when squeezed but its zest, much like its leaves, impart a subtle but inimitable flavour when added to a dish.

Mustard seeds These tiny black seeds are an essential spice in South Indian cooking. They are tempered with a dose of hot oil, mustard seeds, curry leaves and sometimes dried red chilli. Mustard seeds have a slightly bitter aftertaste and this quality makes them perfect for adding to pickles.

Oyster sauce Made from boiled oysters and seasoning, this rich, savoury sauce is an important ingredient in Chinese cooking, especially in meat and vegetable stir-fries and stews.

Palm sugar

Pandan leaf

Preserved soy bean paste

Rice vermicelli

Roasted grated coconut

Salam leaf

Sour star fruit

Soy sauce

Star anise

Palm sugar Palm sugar, or *gula melaka* to Malay-speakers, is made from the sap of the palm tree. Fresh palm sap is boiled down shortly after collection to make a concentrated heavy palm syrup. This syrup is poured into bamboo sections to form cylindrical shapes, or into small shallow bowls to form shallow hemispheres. The sugar ranges from almost white to pale honey-gold to a deep, dark brown, with varying consistency. Palm sugar is used in Southeast Asian cuisine in both savoury and sweet dishes.

Pandan leaf The long, narrow pandan leaf is also known as *pandanus* leaf. They are used in both savoury and sweet dishes in Malaysia, Singapore, Indonesia and Thailand. This leaf, with its delicate flavour, is as essential to Asian cooking as vanilla is to Western cooking. The leaves can be used whole and are also pounded and strained to lend flavour and colour to sweets.

Preserved soy bean paste Better known as *tau cheo* to Hokkien-speakers or *taucu* to Malay-speakers, preserved soy bean paste was first used as a flavouring agent by early Chinese cooks. Over time, cooks in Southeast Asia, including Singapore, Malaysia and Thailand, discovered the versatility of these salty beans and began to add them to their dishes. These beans are sometimes used whole but mostly mashed before they are added to a dish. They are also typically countered with a pinch of sugar for a better balance of flavours.

Rice vermicelli Rice vermicelli is sold dried or fresh. Made from ground rice, these noodles are also known as *bee hoon* in Hokkien. Dried rice vermicelli have a long shelf life and can be kept for a few months is stored well. It has to be soaked in water or scalded in hot water and drained to soften before used in cooking.

Roasted grated coconut Roasted grated coconut is often added to enrich certain dishes. This is obtained by roasting fresh grated coconut, stirring constantly, in a dry pan over low heat until it turns golden brown. If desiccated coconut is used, the flesh should be moistened with a little water before roasting. However, desiccated coconut lacks the rich flavour of fresh coconut.

Kerisik is obtained by grating the flesh of a mature coconut, roasting it until golden brown and then pounding or grinding it until the oil seeps out. If fresh coconut is unavailable, desiccated coconut can be used instead.

Salam leaf The tough, aromatic salam leaf, similar in shape and size to the bay leaf, contains volatile oils. The fresh leaves are used whole in Indonesian curries to impart a unique flavour. If *salam* leaves are unavailable they may be substituted with curry leaves or bay leaves, which are somewhat similar in flavour.

Sour star fruit Known to Malay-speakers as *belimbing buluh*, this small green, elongated fruit is a relative of the more famous yellow star fruit but it is extremely sour and is used predominantly in cooking. Sour star fruit, when added in small quantities, imparts a tartness to the dish. It is sometimes also known as sour finger carambola. If sour star fruit is unavailable, replace with segments of lime.

Soy sauce Soy sauce, used to flavour and colour food, is made from salted soy beans. There are three types of soy sauce. Light soy sauce is the type most commonly used for flavouring. Dark soy sauce (pictured) is a black, thick sauce with a stronger flavour. It is generally used in stews for its flavour and colour. Sweet soy sauce is a thick, sweet sauce used in dishes of Javanese origin.

Star anise Star anise comes from a tree belonging to the magnolia family. The dried eight-pointed star-shaped seed pod is used for flavouring meat and poultry dishes in Malaysia, Singapore, Indonesia (*bunga lawang*), China (*baht gok*) and Vietnam (*hoi*).

Stink beans

Sweet leaf

Tamarind pulp

Torch ginger bud

Turmeric

Turmeric leaf

Turmeric powder

White sesame seeds

Stink beans Also known as bitter bean, *petai* in Malaysia and Indonesia and *sataw* in Thailand, stink beans have a distinctive flavour and are typically added to stir-fries and curries. They are sold in bunches with the beans still in the pods or shelled.

Sweet leaf Known as *pucuk manis* to Malay-speakers, this green leafy vegetable has a sweet, slightly nutty taste. It is typically added to stir-fries, soups and salads in Malaysian and Indonesian cooking.

Tamarind pulp This dark brown, sticky pulp is gathered from pods of the tamarind plant, and within the pulp are many hard seeds. Tamarind pulp is typically used to make tamarind juice, which imparts a sour flavour to dishes. Tamarind juice is made by mixing a portion of the pulp with water and then straining it. The pulp is rarely used as it is, except when it is part of a marinade.

Torch ginger bud Torch ginger bud, which has a delicate aroma, is the flower of a tall and aromatic ginger native to Southeast Asia. In Indonesia, where it is called *kecombrong*, it is cooked with fish to reduce the smell or sliced as part of a vegetable salad. In Malaysia, it is known as *bunga kantan* or *bunga siantan*. In Thailand the flowers (*kaalaa*) are served raw with *nam prik*.

Turmeric Also known as yellow ginger, turmeric is used both for its flavour and its ability to colour a dish bright yellow. It tastes somewhat like a warmer, spicier version of ginger. Some people have even described it as bitter. Handle the orangey yellow flesh of turmeric with care because its juice is notorious for leaving stubborn stains, whether on your fingers, clothes, chopping board or counter top.

Turmeric leaf This large leaf is used in Malaysia, Singapore and Indonesia for flavouring food.

Turmeric powder Turmeric powder is derived from ground, dried turmeric. To Malay-speakers, it is known as *serbuk kunyit*, which means yellow powder, an indication of its deep yellow pigment. Turmeric powder is an essential component of curry powder.

White sesame seeds These tear-drop shaped seeds are mainly used to garnish and flavour dishes. They have a distinct flavour, which is enhanced when roasted. In Asian cooking, white sesame seeds are toasted without oil and left to brown slightly. They are then added as a garnish after the dish is cooked. Vary the amount added to your personal preference.

WEIGHTS & MEASURES

Quantities for this book are given in Metric, Imperial and American (spoon and cup) measures. Standard spoon and cup measurements used are: 1 tsp = 5 ml, 1 Tbsp = 15 ml, 1 cup = 250 ml. All measures are level unless otherwise stated.

Liquid And Volume Measures

Metric	Imperial	American
5 ml	$1/6$ fl oz	1 teaspoon
10 ml	$1/3$ fl oz	1 dessertspoon
15 ml	$1/2$ fl oz	1 tablespoon
60 ml	2 fl oz	$1/4$ cup (4 tablespoons)
85 ml	$2^1/2$ fl oz	$1/3$ cup
90 ml	3 fl oz	$3/8$ cup (6 tablespoons)
125 ml	4 fl oz	$1/2$ cup
180 ml	6 fl oz	$3/4$ cup
250 ml	8 fl oz	1 cup
300 ml	10 fl oz ($1/2$ pint)	$1^1/4$ cups
375 ml	12 fl oz	$1^1/2$ cups
435 ml	14 fl oz	$1^3/4$ cups
500 ml	16 fl oz	2 cups
625 ml	20 fl oz (1 pint)	$2^1/2$ cups
750 ml	24 fl oz ($1^1/5$ pints)	3 cups
1 litre	32 fl oz ($1^3/5$ pints)	4 cups
1.25 litres	40 fl oz (2 pints)	5 cups
1.5 litres	48 fl oz ($2^2/5$ pints)	6 cups
2.5 litres	80 fl oz (4 pints)	10 cups

Oven Temperature

	°C	°F	Gas Regulo
Very slow	120	250	1
Slow	150	300	2
Moderately slow	160	325	3
Moderate	180	350	4
Moderately hot	190/200	375/400	5/6
Hot	210/220	410/425	6/7
Very hot	230	450	8
Super hot	250/290	475/550	9/10

Dry Measures

Metric	Imperial
30 grams	1 ounce
45 grams	$1^1/2$ ounces
55 grams	2 ounces
70 grams	$2^1/2$ ounces
85 grams	3 ounces
100 grams	$3^1/2$ ounces
110 grams	4 ounces
125 grams	$4^1/2$ ounces
140 grams	5 ounces
280 grams	10 ounces
450 grams	16 ounces (1 pound)
500 grams	1 pound, $1^1/2$ ounces
700 grams	$1^1/2$ pounds
800 grams	$1^3/4$ pounds
1 kilogram	2 pounds, 3 ounces
1.5 kilograms	3 pounds, $4^1/2$ ounces
2 kilograms	4 pounds, 6 ounces

Length

Metric	Imperial
0.5 cm	$1/4$ in
1 cm	$1/2$ in
1.5 cm	$3/4$ in
2.5 cm	1 in

Abbreviation

tsp	teaspoon
Tbsp	tablespoon
g	gram
kg	kilogram
ml	millilitre